Basic
MARATHON TRAINING

All the Technique and Gear You Need to Get Started

Leigh Ann Berry, editor

Don Garber,
marathon coach and consultant

Photographs by
Chip Mitchell

STACKPOLE
BOOKS

0 11557 03114 0

Published by
STACKPOLE BOOKS
5067 Ritter Road
Mechanicsburg, PA 17055
www.stackpolebooks.com

Printed in China

10 9 8 7 6 5 4 3 2 1

FIRST EDITION

All photographs © 2004 Chip Mitchell, www.chipmitchell.com, except as follows: Alan Wycheck: 17–22, 23 (two watches, shoe inserts, sunscreen), 24 (all except whistle tucked into pants), 30, 41, 42 (left), 75; Bettmann/CORBIS: 5, 45; Ed Bock Photography, Inc./CORBIS: 6; Julian Hirshowitz/CORBIS: 36; AFP/CORBIS: 67; Lee Snider/CORBIS: 73

Cover design by Tracy Patterson

Library of Congress Cataloging-in-Publication Data

Basic marathon training : all the techniques and equipment you need to get started / Leigh Ann Berry, editor.— 1st ed.
    p. cm.
"Don Garber, marathon coach and consultant ; photographs by Chip Mitchell."
ISBN 0-8117-3114-6
 1. Marathon running—Training.
GV1065.17.T73 B37 2004
796.42'52—dc22
                                2003022286

Contents

Acknowledgments

Many people deserve thanks for their assistance in creating this book. First and foremost is contributor Don Garber, whose experience and knowledge provide the core of the information presented in these pages. Don has been a runner for more than thirty years and has completed eighteen marathons. Through his coaching with the Leukemia and Lymphoma Society's Team in Training program and the Richmond YMCA's Marathon Training Team, he has helped hundreds of runners successfully complete their own first marathons. We are truly fortunate to be able to distill his coaching advice into book form. Thanks also go to Don's colleague Joe Zielinski for his contributions.

Photographer Chip Mitchell's skill was invaluable in capturing the runners in action. His organization and professionalism helped make the photo shoot go smoothly. I especially want to thank our photo models who gave up many hours of a Saturday to participate in the shoot: Carrie Burton, Chris Engel, Kara Gallagher, Vicki and John Green, Faith Hect, Frits Huntjens, John Johnson, Laurie Shinn, Michelle and Tim Van Meter, and Katherine Zampolin. Special thanks also go to coach Mike Davi and the Richmond branch of the Virginia Chapter of Team in Training.

Photographer Alan Wycheck's expertise provided the still shots of running clothing and equipment that appear in chapter 4. A special thanks to Henry Klugh, manager of The Inside Track running store in Harrisburg, Pennsylvania, for his generosity in providing access to his inventory and to his employee, Tim Skoczen, for his assistance and advice in selecting which items to photograph.

A very special thanks to Hal Higdon for graciously allowing us to reprint his training program on page 27. I have followed Hal's programs for all five of my marathons and I am a true believer in his sensible, achievable schedule. Thanks also to the Road Runners Club of America for permitting us to use their safety and etiquette tips.

My personal thanks also to the runners in my own life who have inspired and encouraged me: Rich Centola, Deb Cooney, Bob Gibson, MaryAnn Kennedy, Bob Rudolph, and Mike Thompson have seen me through my own marathon training and have shared thousands of happy miles on the roads with me. Their wisdom and knowledge have helped form the basis for my own.

—Leigh Ann Berry

Introduction

To some people, the idea of running 26.2 miles is as far-fetched as climbing Mount Everest or swimming across the English Channel. But over the past few years more and more people have come to realize that not only is running a marathon achievable, but that training to complete the event can actually be an enjoyable and immensely fulfilling experience. Welcome to the new running boom of the early twenty-first century.

I am a poster child for this new era of marathoners. Basically sedentary through high school and college, I began running in 1996 as a means of losing weight and getting fit. After completing a few local 5K and 10K races, by 1998 I felt I was ready for a bigger challenge. In January I signed up for the Leukemia and Lymphoma Society's Team in Training program, and with the assistance and encouragement of a coach and a supportive group of fellow runners, I trained for and completed the Marine Corps Marathon in October 1998.

Prior to my first marathon I had never considered myself to be anything more than a recreational runner; I certainly never thought of myself as an athlete. But as running legend Dr. George Sheehan so aptly said, "Everyone is an athlete. The only difference is that some of us are in training, and some are not."

You, too, can become a marathoner. If you are ready for the challenge and are willing to put in the time and training it takes, you can prepare yourself to undertake this life-altering experience. Many people find that it changes their lives in dramatically positive ways. Not only will you become fitter and physically feel better about yourself, but you will also gain self-confidence and perseverance that will serve you in good stead throughout every aspect of your life.

We hope that this book will provide you with the basic information you will need to get from the first day of your training through to the finish line and beyond. While a book can never replace the personal assistance of an actual running coach or supply the camaraderie of training with a group of like-minded runners, it will supplement your knowledge and give you a basis from which you can begin to develop your training program. It is our hope that you will learn from the basics presented in these pages and then seek out a coach or more experienced runner in your area with whom you can continue your training. The Resources section on page 79 provides information on how to find such groups throughout the country.

1

Why Run?

Benefits of Running

For longtime runners, you could just as well ask, "Why breathe?" or "Why eat?" as "Why run?" For some people, running is such an integral part of their lives that they no longer stop and ask themselves why they do it. But for those who have not yet discovered the pleasure and fulfillment that running can bring, here is a summary of three of the greatest benefits you will experience from running:

1. INCREASED PHYSICAL HEALTH

Running will make you fitter. It's that simple. When you get off the couch and out onto the roads or trails, you force your body to adapt to a new set of physical requirements. If you have been primarily a sedentary person up until now, it is essential that you start out slowly. By gradually increasing the degree of intensity or duration of each running session, you will slowly but surely begin to see improvements in your physical condition.

volume of blood with each heartbeat. The increased quantity of blood flowing through your heart and veins helps clear out some of the deposits of plaque that build up on the walls of veins and arteries, and even encourages the blood vessels to grow in size and number.

But what does all this mean on a practical level? If you make the commitment to starting and sticking with a running program, what can you look forward to? Here are just a few of the specific physical benefits of running:

- You will lose fat and your muscles will become more toned, meaning that your clothes will fit better.
- You will be able to breathe more easily, not only when you are running, but also when doing everyday activities such as climbing stairs or carrying groceries.
- Your blood pressure and resting heart rate will decrease.

Running is considered an aerobic activity. This means that it causes your body to use more oxygen. It is also a cardiovascular activity, which means that it requires the heart to pump blood faster to circulate this oxygen throughout the body. As you gain fitness, your heart will become more efficient, pumping a greater

- You will gain better flexibility and range of motion.
- You will sleep better and have more energy .
- Your skin and hair will look healthier.

With physical improvements such as these, who wouldn't want to start running right away? But if you still need more convincing, keep reading.

2. IMPROVED MENTAL HEALTH

Some runners would say that the psychological benefits of running outweigh even the most significant physical benefits. While more difficult to quantify, the mental benefits of running are undeniable. The increased sense of well-being that running brings is actually the result of a chemical reaction: when you run, your body increases the production of hormones known as endorphins. These chemicals are responsible for the "high" that some runners experience during or after a run.

Running also significantly decreases stress levels. After a hectic or stressful day at the office, most runners can hardly wait to get home and out the door again for a run. Running clears the head and calms the soul. For some, it also provides a rare time of quiet reflection and a chance to process the day's events and think through challenging situations. For others, it offers an opportunity to clear the mind of all other pressing concerns. For these runners, the only concern is getting from the start to the finish; all other considerations are for the moment insignificant. Running can be a great release.

A third psychological benefit of running is an increased sense of self-confidence. In general, runners tend to be happier, more confident people. Not only does the improved physical condition bring with it an improved self-image, but you also gain a sense of pride and confidence in your ability as an athlete. When you can rely on your body to carry you from the start to the finish of a run, be it 6 miles or 26.2, you gain an incredible amount of self-confidence. You can apply this confidence to all aspects of your life. Many new runners find that they are inspired to embrace new challenges in their jobs, accept new responsibilities, or strive for new goals in other areas of their lives.

3. ENHANCED SOCIAL INTERACTION

The social benefits of running offer a third great reason to make this activity a part of your life. One of the greatest joys of being a runner is the chance to share your passion with millions of others around the world. The moment you take that first step, you join a community of fellow runners who are just as enthusiastic as you are—or more so. Find some of these people in your local area, and try to run with them at least once a week if you can.

Coach's Tip: You can find fellow runners through your local Road Runners Club of America (RRCA) chapter (see page 80 for details) or through your local gym or YMCA. You can also gain instant access to a running community by signing up for a charity running group such as Team in Training. See chapter 5 for more information on training with others.

The sense of camaraderie and belonging that comes from running with a group cannot be denied. Although some runners say they prefer solitude, most treasure the runs they share with others and rely on their companions for support and encouragement.

The Running Boom Begins

The year is 1980. Jim Fixx's *Second Book of Running* (a follow-up to his best-selling *Complete Book of Running*, published three years earlier) has just been published. Thousands of people are discovering competitive running as a sport. Almost all of these new runners are fit, relatively young men. They see running as a way to push themselves further and test the limits of their endurance. Getting in shape is a great side benefit, but it may not be the primary motivation. Inspired by American men such as Bill Rodgers and Frank Shorter (whose 1972 gold medal at the Olympic Games in Munich spawned an initial U.S. running boom in the previous decade), these men enter local 5K and 10K races in droves and launch an entire industry of running gear and equipment. More than a few of these runners choose the marathon as the ultimate test of their endurance. In 1980, approximately 120,000 runners completed marathons; 89.5 percent of those finishers were men. The median time for a men's marathon in 1980 was 3:32:17 and for a women's was 4:03:39.*

All median times taken from the USA Track & Field Road Running Information Center, www.runningusa.org.

The New Running Boom

Fast-forward almost two decades. The year is 1998. A book called *The Non-Runner's Marathon Trainer*, by David A. Whitsett, has just been published. Runners of all shapes, sizes, and abilities are discovering the joy of running. The participants in this "second running boom," as it is known, look markedly different from those of the first. More and more women are lining up at local races and swelling the ranks of local running clubs. Both men and women turn to running as a means to lose weight, stay in shape, and meet new people. The goal of these runners is not necessarily to win races, but just to compete. As the self-styled spokesman for this group, *Runner's World* magazine columnist John "The Penguin" Bingham says: "The miracle isn't that I finished. . . . The miracle is that I had the courage to start."

A phenomenon known as charity running also helps bring many runners to the marathon distance. Through programs such as the Arthritis Foundation's Joints in Motion, the American Diabetes Association's Team Diabetes, and the Leukemia and Lymphoma Society's Team in Training, runners receive coaching and train with a group of people to prepare for one of a selection of national marathons. The goal for the bulk of these first-time marathoners is simply to finish. Fueled by this new influx of participants, by 1998, 419,000 runners complete marathons; 34 percent of those finishers are women. The median time for this second running boom illustrates the shift in focus: by 1995, it had risen to 3:54 for men and 4:15 for women.

Among the participants in the New Running Boom are many first-time marathoners, such as those who train with groups like the Leukemia and Lymphoma Society's Team in Training.

3

Team in Training coaches plan the weekly long run.

To this day, the second running boom continues unabated. After a drop in participation in 2001 following the September 11 terrorist attacks, marathoners returned to the roads in full force in 2002. An estimated 450,000 people completed a marathon in 2002; the percentage of female finishers increased to 40 percent. The median time for the finishers also continued to increase: to 4:20:01 for men and 4:56:46 for women. Clearly, this new generation of marathoners is a very different group than those who participated twenty years ago.

The surge in participation is not without its critics. For many longtime runners who continue to run competitively, the huge numbers of slower runners on the course can be seen as an obstacle rather than accomplishment. The competition for race entries to some of the more popular national marathons, such as the Marine Corps and New York City events, has forced organizers to use a lottery system to award entries. Many competitive runners express frustration that they can no longer gain entry into some of the larger races because a set number of spots are automatically reserved for charity runners.

Despite such complaints, it appears that the new running boom is here to stay. With the proper guidance and information, these new runners can become more than just one-time marathon finishers. They can become lifelong runners who enjoy all the physical, mental, and social benefits that running has to offer.

2

Why Run a Marathon?

The Marathon and Its History

The marathon has long held a fascination for runners and nonrunners alike. The 26.2-mile distance has come to represent the ultimate achievement of road running. Although ultramarathons offer longer distances and triathlons a variety of different sports, nothing has unseated the marathon as the challenge of choice for most distance runners.

The marathon as a competitive event traces its history to 1896. The first modern Olympic Games, held in Athens, Greece, staged a long-distance race to celebrate the run of Pheidippides, a Greek messenger who in 490 B.C., delivered a desperate call for help from an Athenian general to the Spartans, some 150 miles away, to come to their aid in a fight against the Persians near the plains of Marathon, on the eastern coast. According to legend, Pheidippides reached Sparta in two days. Although the Spartans did not arrive in time to help, the Athenians were victorious. According to legend, Pheidippides was again dispatched to deliver a message, this time from the plains of Marathon into Athens, a distance of roughly 25 miles. Unfortunately—and much to the chagrin of modern-day marathon runners—after delivering the news of the victory, Pheidippides collapsed and died.

The Boston Marathon is the world's oldest continuously held marathon. Pictured here are runners coming through the streets of Framingham, Massachusetts, 30 minutes after the start of the 1925 marathon.

In running a marathon, you really only need to compete with yourself.

Whether the legend has any truth to it is a matter of dispute. Many modern historians doubt the verity of the story, citing the fact that the messenger is hardly mentioned in contemporary accounts of the battle. Nevertheless, it does make for a good story and served as the source for a now-famous quip by a modern running legend, Frank Shorter, who remarked to a fellow runner at Mile 21 of a 1971 marathon, "Why couldn't Pheidippides have died here?"

The 25-mile distance became the standard for the running of the marathon at the 1896 Athens Games. The race ran from the plains of Marathon into the city of Athens, where it finished in the Olympic stadium. The winner was a Greek runner, Spiridon Louis, who beat the other competitors to win the gold medal with a time of 2 hours, 58 minutes, 50 seconds. Among the other runners represented that day were members of the Boston Athletic Association, whose team manager, John

Graham, was so impressed by the Athens Olympic marathon that he staged one in Boston the next year. In 1897, fifteen competitors lined up for the first running of the Boston Athletic Association Marathon, an event that continues to this day and is the oldest continuously held marathon.

The 25-mile distance continued to be the standard until the 1908 Olympics, when the British designed a marathon course that started at Windsor Castle and finished in the Olympic stadium. The length of this course, 26 miles and 385 yards, became the standard distance for the Olympic marathon event and was gradually adopted as the universal standard for all marathons.

Why People Run Marathons

People run marathons for a multitude of different reasons: the chance to accomplish something extraordinary, to push oneself beyond the limits of normal endurance, and to experience the thrill of triumphing over adversity seem to be among the most common motivations. Finishing a marathon brings a sense of elation that few other life experiences can produce. The sense of accomplishment is tremendous; some marathon finishers are inspired to achieve goals in other aspects of their lives that they had previously thought were unattainable. People run marathons because they have some inkling that it will change their lives. They might not know how it will change them, exactly, but they know that their lives will be altered by the experience.

One of the joys of marathon running is that while you are competing along with hundreds or thousands of other runners, you really only need to compete with yourself. Although some veteran marathoners strive to win age-group awards, the vast majority of runners are essentially racing themselves, setting goals based upon their previous personal bests (also known as personal records or PRs) or around time considerations such as qualifying for the Boston Marathon.

While your goal for your first marathon should simply be to finish the race happy and healthy, should you decide to continue with marathoning, you can decide for yourself how you want to approach your next race. You certainly could continue running marathons just to finish, with no expectations of a finishing time. Indeed, John "The Penguin" Bingham extols the virtues of this approach in his monthly column in *Runner's World*. His growing popularity raises the possibility that marathon running could perhaps become a popular hobby.

It does seem that marathoning has some sort of addictive quality; many runners complete their first marathons and almost immediately start making plans for their next race. Once you experience the thrill of crossing the finish line, you can't help but want to go back to experience that feeling again. Although nothing ever quite compares with the first time, each subsequent marathon offers its own set of challenges: the course, the weather, how well you are trained. All of these factors make marathoning a perpetually new experience and may explain why even veteran marathon runners can still get excited about the prospect of doing the distance yet again.

All this is not to minimize the fact that training for and completing a marathon is actually a difficult, physically demanding task. But, as the old saying goes, if it were easy, everyone would be doing it. Although more and more people train for marathons each year, that does not mean it is becoming easier. True, training programs have been made more manageable in recent years, and it's possible to train for a marathon and still maintain your role as a full-time employee, spouse, parent, or all three of the above. But marathon training does require a serious commitment of time and effort. If you don't feel that you can devote the time to putting in long runs during the weekend as well as several hours for shorter runs during the week, perhaps you should reevaluate whether now is a good time for you to be undertaking this challenge. Other running goals provide a similar challenge and reward but are less time-consuming. Many people who don't have the time or energy to commit to training for a full marathon opt instead to train for one of the growing number of half-marathons (13.1-mile races) throughout the country. Then, if they still wish to pursue the full marathon, they can do so at another point in their lives.

But if you know that you are ready, willing, and able to commit the time and effort to preparing yourself for this amazing challenge, your hard work will be rewarded tenfold. So keep reading and get ready to become a marathoner!

3

The Basics

Becoming a Runner: Form and Breathing

If you are not currently a runner, it's important to first discover a little more about running in general before you jump into learning about marathon equipment and training. Although running may be perceived as physically demanding, few sports come as naturally to human beings as running does. Not everyone has perfect form or mechanics, but most people can easily develop them once they know what works best.

Go to the high school track or a local road race and watch other runners in action. Concentrate on their form and posture, and make note of the variations you see. You will probably witness just about every style imaginable, from long legged arm swingers to those who run hunched over and hardly swing their arms at all. You will probably also be able to pick out runners who look natural and graceful. These are the runners who are inherently exhibiting good running form. These are the runners that you want to emulate.

Now go out and run a little yourself. Not too far—just enough to allow you to notice what you do when you run. Don't try to consciously make any changes. If you can have someone videotape you as you run, that's even better. When you watch the tape, you will be able

to see how you carry your body, swing your arms, and move your legs. No two runners will have exactly the same form, but a few points are consistent enough to mention: Keep your head up and your body erect. Not only will this improve your form, but it will also help ease your breathing. Hold your arms naturally at your sides and let them swing from front to back. Don't clench your fists. Take smooth, even strides. Don't bounce up and down. Use your toes to push off and move your body forward.

Breathing is another major factor. Oxygen is an essential element of running. Because it is an aerobic activity, running requires you to breathe faster and more heavily to draw greater quantities of oxygen into your lungs. For the beginner, breathing can often create one of the biggest challenges. If you find that you are having trouble breathing as you run, slow down. Your pace should be such that you are able to speak to a fellow runner while you are running. If you can't, you're running too fast. Make sure that you are taking full, deep breaths. You will probably fall into a regular rhythm of breathing as you run without even being aware of it. Running expert Dr. Jack Daniels has studied breathing patterns (as well as just about every other aspect of running physiology) and noted that most runners breathe on a 2–2 ratio to their footfalls: they inhale for 2 steps, then exhale for 2 steps. Slower runners can breathe in a 3–3 pattern, while runners at the end of a race sprinting toward the finish often shift to a 2–1 pattern.

Coach's Tip: A common problem that plagues beginners is the dreaded side stitch: a sharp pain under the rib cage or in the lower side that makes breathing difficult and can practically cause you to double over in pain. Although theories abound as to what causes it, even Dr. Daniels admits that he doesn't really know for sure. The best thing to do to try to eliminate side stitches is to change your breathing pattern. If you normally breathe on a 2–2 pattern, switch to a 3–3 rhythm to try to get rid of the pain.

The Physiology of Running

When it comes to fitness sports, none is simpler than running. There are no challenging moves to learn or stances to perfect; running is simply putting one foot in front of the other and moving forward. But although running might seem simple on the surface, as with all physiological functions, what goes on beneath the surface is far more complex.

In order to run, the body goes through a complicated process of musculoskeletal contractions to propel itself forward. To fuel this process, the body uses energy that is derived from the chemical breakdown of carbohydrates (see chapter 6 for more details on turning carbohydrates into energy). Two different types of muscles, known as slow-twitch and fast-twitch muscles, cooperate to accomplish this task. Long-distance runners rely primarily on slow-twitch muscle fibers, while sprinters use primarily fast-twitch muscles. But through training strategies such as speedwork (see page 33), you can train your body to use both types of muscles to improve your strength and efficiency as a runner.

Coach's Tip: According to the dictionary, running is the act of moving "at a rapid pace so that both feet are off the ground together for part of each stride." This definition lies at the heart of what distinguishes running from fast walking. No matter how fast you walk, at least one foot is always (or should always be) firmly planted on the ground.

Running Economy

Just about anyone can run, but not everyone knows how to run efficiently. Running economy is the measure of how efficiently your body uses energy throughout the run. Your body has a fixed amount of stored energy to use, and how you apply that energy during a run or road race will directly correlate to how far and how fast you can run. A number of different factors affect running economy. Here are the main ones and how you can adjust them to make yourself a more efficient runner:

- **Posture.** Maintain an upright but relaxed posture. Keep your head erect. Keep your neck, shoulders, arms, and hands relaxed. If you feel yourself starting to tighten up, especially during a long run, roll your neck and shoulders and shake out your arms and hands to relax them.

Keep your body upright but relaxed while running.

- **Arm Movement.** Keep your arms and hands moving from front to back, not from side to side. Use the momentum of your arms to help propel you forward. Imagine holding 16- to 18-inch batons in your hands. Don't stab yourself in the thighs with the batons; hold them to your side. Keep your arm motion relaxed and your hands loose and comfortable. Pretend you are holding a potato chip between the middle finger and thumb of each hand as you run.

Hands should be at your sides, moving from front to back.

- **Stride Length and Rate.** As your mileage increases, you will naturally fall into a stride length and rate that are most comfortable for you. Generally, smaller steps and a quicker turnover (the rate at which you pick up and put down your feet) are more efficient than a longer, slower stride. Try to imagine that your legs are like a wheel rolling along, not two pogo sticks that bounce along the road. Most runners take at least 160 steps in a minute; elite runners take more than 180! Measure your own stride rate to see where it falls. When running up hills, take smaller steps and keep your leg turnover the same.

  In essence, a proper stride is the one that feels the most comfortable. The more relaxed you are, and the less you force a particular stride, the better you'll run and the less chance you'll have of getting injured.

- **Footstrike.** Notice how your foot lands when it hits the ground. Ideally, it should land heel-first and then roll forward so the foot can push off for the next step with the toes. If your feet don't strike in this manner—if you are a midfoot or toe striker—you need to compensate for this by choosing proper shoes or seeing a podiatrist for custom-made orthotic inserts. Not only can footstrike problems decrease running economy, but they can cause injury as well.

Your foot should land heel-first and then roll forward.

External factors can also affect running economy. Though you can't make physical changes to improve these things, you can make choices:

- **Running Surface.** In training, when you have the option, run on softer, smooth surfaces. Concrete is worst; grass and dirt are best. Macadam and asphalt are somewhere in between. The hard impact of the road reduces running economy.

- **Drafting.** Headwinds can dramatically affect running economy. A 3 mph headwind can affect performance up to 2 percent, while a 9 mph headwind can affect performance up to 8 percent. When running or racing in groups, it is perfectly fine to "tuck" in behind another runner. But be sure to take turns so everyone can benefit from the advantage.

Hitting the Roads

Now that you've learned a little bit about the mechanics of running, it's time to put them into practice by actually getting out and running. If you've never run before, you might not have the first idea how you should go about starting your training program. Chapter 5 will give you more details on distances and schedules, but even more basic than that is where you should run and when.

The beauty of running is that with the right shoes, most people can just head out the front door and start running. Although this might be more of a challenge depending on where you live, as long as you have access to roads with a decent berm, you have an almost unlimited territory on which to put in your training miles. You will probably first want to get in the car and scout out a few good beginning routes. Measure the distance on your car's odometer and make a mental note of the condition and safety of each road. If possible, choose roads that don't have a high volume of traffic, but for safety's sake, avoid roads that are completely isolated. Also try to avoid roads with a steep drop-off from the edge to the berm. Running on this slant, or camber, can cause or aggravate knee and hip problems. Run on the most even part of the road. Out-and-back courses are often the easiest to measure, but longer loops provide greater variety. Choose a number of different routes and alternate between them. You can also find wonderful running courses in urban parks or along trails. These locations are often frequented by other runners and not only can provide a safe, traffic-free place to run, but also can be a great way to meet other runners who may be training for a marathon. Contact your local running club to ask about the best running locations in your area.

The question of when to run is a very personal one. Each person has to consider his or her own schedule and carve out the time to make running fit into his or her own life. Some people find that running first thing in the morning works best for them and love the solitude and peace of the early morning. Others with the luxury of more flexible schedules or understanding workplaces can run during the lunch hour. Still others prefer to run in the evening to work off the stress of the day.

You should speak with the other members of your family to discuss how your marathon training will affect them. Will you need to ask your spouse to make dinner on the evenings that you are scheduled to do training runs? Will you need to do homework earlier in the evening? Can you ask your mother-in-law to watch the kids in the morning while you do your long weekend run? You can also involve family members in your runs. Invite your spouse to bike along with you for a long run on a flat trail, or buy a baby jogger to take

Coach's Tip: Take advantage of current technology to help measure your distance on courses you're running for the first time. Pedometers measure distance with a reasonable degree of accuracy and can be purchased for around $125 (cheaper ones may be available but are not generally not very accurate). These devices are great for first-time runners who run by time but still want to know what distance they've covered.

your children along. Not only will this help your family members feel like they are participating in your training, but it will also set an example and get them more interested in their own fitness.

However you choose to do so, make sure that you actually schedule a time of day to run—write it down in your daily planner or enter it into a Personal Digital Assistant. That way you will consider your running just as important a commitment as a scheduled haircut appointment or meeting with the financial planner.

Safety

Compared with the perils of cycling or open-water swimming, running is a fairly safe sport. But like any other activity, the choices you make can either increase or jeopardize your personal safety. Be conscious of the world around you when you are out running, whether you are on or off the roads. At times, the sheer joy of running or—at the opposite end of the spectrum—the fatigue of a long run can make staying alert to outside

dangers more difficult. By following these basic guidelines, you will have a much better chance of staying safe:

- Run against traffic so you can see cars approach you rather than have cars coming from behind.
- Even when you do run against traffic, look over your shoulder if you hear traffic coming from behind to make sure someone isn't using your lane to pass another car.
- Do not wear headphones. You need your ears to be aware of your surroundings. Headphones are acceptable only when running inside on a treadmill.
- Wear reflective material if you run before dawn or after dark.
- When approaching an intersection, make eye contact with a driver who is waiting to proceed onto the main road. If you aren't sure he or she sees you, pass behind the car.
- Carry identification or write your name, phone number, and blood type on the inside sole of your running shoe.
- Tell someone where you are running, or leave a note stating the direction and duration of your run.

Additional safety tips for women can be found on page 47.

Top: *Run against traffic so you can see oncoming cars.* Bottom: *Identification, such as this Road ID™, can also be worn on the outside of your shoes.*

4

Equipment

Unlike some other sports and hobbies in which you need to commit lots of money up front to purchase equipment or accessories, running really only requires an investment in a good pair of shoes. There are, however, a lot of optional clothes and accessories that can help make running more comfortable and enjoyable. These little extras can be especially important when putting in the long hours required to train for a marathon.

Shoes

The most important thing you can do to stay healthy and to enjoy your running is to train in a proper pair of running shoes. If you are only running 2 or 3 miles around the neighborhood, you might be able, for the short term, to get by wearing any shoes. But as you increase your mileage, you will also be increasing the stress on your body. Your feet bear the brunt of the impact when they hit the ground, so it's essential to wear a shoe that is designed to support your foot properly.

There are several important considerations when selecting the proper running shoe. The first of these is the type of foot you have, based on your arch. The best way to determine which of the three you have is to wet the bottom of your foot and step onto a piece of dark paper or fabric. Compare the imprint your foot makes to the three on the next page.

Normal Arch: The area connecting the front of your foot and your heel is relatively wide. It should be about a third as wide as the front of your foot.

High Arch: The area connecting the front of your foot and your heel is almost nonexistent.

Flat Foot: The area connecting the front of your foot and your heel is very wide—in some cases almost as wide as the front of your foot.

The other factor affecting shoe choice is less obvious and has to do with how your foot responds when it hits the ground. Pronation is the natural tendency of your foot to roll inward and flatten out before it rotates outward and prepares to push off again. People with low arches (flat feet) tend to overpronate. Overpronators' feet roll inward too much, and they can suffer from knee and Achilles tendon problems. Overpronation is far more common than the opposite condition, oversupination, which happens to a few people with high arches whose feet don't pronate enough, but roll outward when they hit the ground. Because the foot is so inflexible and does not absorb shock, supinators often have ankle or shin problems or stress fractures. Supinators' shoes typically wear along the outside edges.

Overpronation and oversupination cannot be corrected through training. Once you are able to determine these two interrelated characteristics, you should start looking for a running shoe that will best suit your needs. On the opposite page are four examples of basic running shoe types and their characteristics. The four categories—cushioned, stability, performance training, and motion control—are taken from *Runner's World* magazine's outstanding online database of shoe reviews available at www.runnersworld.com.

These four shoes are just a sampling of the dozens that are available. The choice of brands, styles, colors, and features of running shoes is almost unlimited. You can typically expect to spend from $65 to $100 or more on a good pair of running shoes.

Coach's Tip: Shoe size in running shoes tends to vary from manufacturer to manufacturer. Often runners will need to buy shoes one-half to one full size larger than their regular casual shoes. A running store shoe salesperson can help you determine which shoe size is best for you.

The best way to make sure that you get the best shoe for your foot type is to go to a store that specializes in running footwear. Look in your local telephone directory under "sporting goods" to find a specialty running store in your area. You will receive much more knowledgeable service from an employee of a specialty store than from a general sporting goods store. Employees of running stores tend to be runners themselves and are usually very good about evaluating your particular needs. If you are a runner already, take along the pair of shoes you have been running in up to now. By looking at how your shoes have worn, a knowledgeable salesperson can gauge how you run and which type of shoe would be best for you. Be sure to also tell the salesperson if you have any current or past injuries or if you wear prescription orthotics in your shoes. Also take along a pair of your running socks to ensure the proper fit.

Coach's Tip: How long your shoes will last is unique to each person. The general rule of thumb is 300 to 500 miles. One thing you can do to make sure your shoes don't have too many miles on them is to remove the innersole and, using a magic marker, write the date you begin running in that pair. Then, by keeping track of your mileage in a running log, you will know approximately how many miles the shoes have on them. It also helps to buy two pairs of the same shoe (once you know for certain that it works well for you) and alternate between them. This will ensure that you have a pair of shoes well broken in for the marathon but still new enough to have sufficient cushioning and support.

CUSHIONED SHOE

Best for runners with normal or high arches who are mild pronators and want a softer, more cushioned ride.

Example: Nike Air Pegasus

STABILITY SHOE

Best for runners with flat feet who may pronate mildly and want a combination of cushioning and stability.

Example: ASICS GT 2000 series (2020, 2040, 2080)

PERFORMANCE TRAINING SHOE

Best for runners with a normal arch who may pronate mildly and want a lightweight shoe to use for racing or training.

Example: Reebok Premier Light

MOTION CONTROL SHOES

Best for runners with flat feet who tend to overpronate and need extra arch support.

Example: Saucony GRID Stabil

Equipment

Three words sum up running clothing: cotton is bad. When you run, in heat or in cold, your comfort will be enhanced by the removal of moisture from your skin. Cotton absorbs moisture and keeps it close to your skin. Synthetic fabrics such as CoolMax or DriFit, however, pull the moisture away from your skin and allow it to evaporate, leaving you dry. These wicking fabrics can be found in shirts, socks, running bras, shorts, and tights. Clothing made from these fabrics tends to be slightly more expensive than traditional cotton running apparel, but it is money well spent.

RUNNING BRA

Women need a high-quality running bra in order to ensure support and comfort. For smaller-chested women, light support is often all that is required, whereas larger cup sizes will probably benefit from a sports bra with compression or perhaps built-in underwire support. Look for a garment that contains CoolMax or a similar moisture-wicking fabric. Seams should be smooth and well finished to avoid chafing.

SHIRTS

Sleeveless, short-sleeved, and long-sleeved noncotton T-shirts are available for runners in countless styles and colors. Tanks (also called singlets) or short-sleeved shirts on their own are best for summer running. Colder weather typically calls for long-sleeved shirts, either on their own or as a base layer under a vest or a jacket. Again, buy garments containing a moisture-wicking fabric.

Equipment

Cold-Weather Running

In cold weather, the best advice for runners is to dress in layers. A base layer of a wicking fabric will pull moisture away from your skin so you won't get chilled. A midlayer such as a T-shirt or fleece will help trap warm air and insulate you against the cold. This layer should also contain a wicking fabric to help move moisture outward. A third, top layer will protect you from rain, snow, or wind and will be moisture's last stop before being released into the air. When it's dry and temperatures are between 30 and 40 degrees Fahrenheit, most runners are comfortable with just a base and a second layer. But when temperatures fall to 0 to 20 degrees or the weather is wet and/or windy, a third layer should be added.

VEST

A vest makes a perfect second layer when the weather is cool but not yet cold. Paired with a long-sleeved T-shirt, a vest offers plenty of warmth and protection.

JACKET

A lightweight running jacket or windbreaker is a good springtime accessory that can be worn over a short- or long-sleeved T-shirt to provide protection from cold, wind, or light rain. Better jackets include features such as mesh vents under arms or across the back to improve breathability.

COLD-WEATHER JACKET

When temperatures drop below 30 degrees or so, it's best to have a reliable outer layer jacket to protect you from rain, snow, or wind. Outer layers are typically made from fabrics such as Gore-Tex that are both waterproof and windproof. Breathability is an important factor when evaluating outer layers; you should consider investing in a garment that keeps heat in but lets perspiration out. Check tags to determine the breathability of the fabric you're considering.

SHORTS

Running shorts are typically designed with a built-in liner (like men's swim trunks) and intended to be worn without underwear underneath. Most shorts feature wicking fabrics that allow moisture to evaporate quickly. Many different lengths and styles are available; try on several pairs to see which you prefer. For the marathon itself, you may want to consider investing in a pair of RaceReady shorts that feature both open mesh pockets and those with Velcro closures. These shorts are perfect for holding gels or other race food as well as hotel keys, car keys, or just about any small item you want to keep with you during the marathon.

Coach's Tip: The most common problem for beginning runners is overdressing. You will generate a lot of body heat when you run, much more than you expect. If you are overdressed, you will not run as well, since your body will be working harder to cool itself. A good rule of thumb is to dress in clothing that you would be comfortable in at a temperature 25 degrees warmer than the actual temperature. For example, if you would go outside in a T-shirt if it were 75 degrees outside, run in a T-shirt if it is 50 degrees.

TIGHTS

Tights can be worn alone or used as a base layer underneath outer pants in colder weather. They offer warmth without being bulky or inhibiting freedom of movement. As with other running garments, look for tights that contain a wicking fabric. Tights come in two styles. Close-fitting, Lycra-based tights (pictured) are similar to leotards. A newer style of loose-fitting tights that provides the same benefits has also become available in recent years. The choice depends on the look and feel that are most comfortable for you.

PANTS

Typically made of nylon or polyester, loose-fitting pants can be worn alone or on top of a base layer. They are also good to wear on cool mornings on the way to a race or training run, to be removed just before you are ready to run. With the availability of tights, fewer and fewer people choose to actually run in pants.

Equipment

REFLECTIVE VEST

A reflective vest is a must-have for runners who train before sunrise or after sunset. Usually made of mesh with adjustable Velcro straps, these vests have high-visibility plastic stripes that reflect cars' headlights and make you more visible to oncoming traffic.

HAT OR VISOR

An important piece of running equipment, a hat can help shade your eyes from sun, rain, or even automobile headlights. Used in conjunction with sunglasses, a hat can help avoid the fatigue caused by squinting in bright sunlight. Most summer running hats are lightweight and well ventilated, allowing heat to escape through side vents. Visors offer an alternative to those who want shaded eyes but not the full coverage of a hat.

COLD-WEATHER HAT

Hats are essential in extremely cold months to help avoid hypothermia. More than 50 percent of body heat is lost through the top of the head. Wearing a hat in cold weather helps preserve this precious heat. Look for a hat made with CoolMax or a similar fabric that will conduct moisture out through the hat and into the air.

COLD-WEATHER PANTS

This outer layer is the bottom half of the cold-weather jacket. These pants are usually made of Gore-Tex or a similar fabric and protect your lower body from rain, snow, and wind. They are usually needed only when it is extremely cold and windy or snowing. Make sure they are large enough to allow for freedom of movement and can comfortably fit over a base layer made of a wicking fabric like CoolMax.

EAR WARMER

For days when it's not quite cold enough for a knit hat, an ear warmer can offer the perfect alternative to going without. Covering the tops of the ears can be just enough to warm you up. And if the temperature rises or you warm up enough to no longer need it, the ear warmer can be easily stuffed in a jacket pocket.

NECK GAITER

For days when it's extremely cold and windy, this simple tube of fabric can help keep the heat from escaping around your neck. Intended to serve the same purpose as a scarf, the neck gaiter can be pulled up over the nose and mouth or tucked down into a jacket for added warmth.

GLOVES

Lightweight gloves can be worn throughout most of the year if the temperatures warrant it. You will see some world-class marathoners come out for fall marathons sporting singlets and briefs but wearing white cotton gloves to keep their hands warm. Colder-weather gloves are usually made of a lightweight thermal fabric that holds in warmth but lets out moisture.

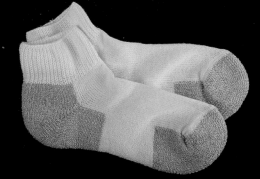

SOCKS

Socks come in as many different varieties as shoes do. Lightweight, extra-cushioned, double-layered, knee-highs, crews, anklets—you may need to experiment with a few different types until you find the kind that is most comfortable for you. Do make sure to purchase a sock that is made from a wicking material such as Cool-Max or DriFit. Not only are wet socks uncomfortable, but they can also cause blisters.

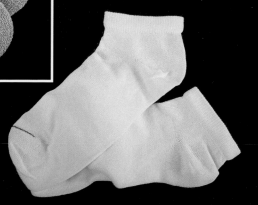

The following running accessories can help make your training safer and more enjoyable:

SUNGLASSES

A good pair of sunglasses is a worthwhile investment if you plan to train in either the summer sun or the glare of winter snow. Not only does squinting causes stress and fatigue, but harmful UV rays can also damage your eyes. Look for a pair that is designed for sports and will fit your face snugly but comfortably.

WATCH

A watch is essential for beginning runners, who usually gauge their training by time rather than by distance. You do not need to buy an overly expensive watch with all the bells and whistles; a basic model with a stopwatch feature will suffice. If you plan to do any track workouts, however, you may want to invest in a model that has a countdown timer feature.

SHOE INSERTS

Shoe inserts are a consideration for heavier runners who may need more cushioning in their shoes or for flat-footed runners who need more arch support. Many different brands and materials are available. Talk to the salesperson at your local running store to help determine which inserts, if any, are best for you.

SUNSCREEN

Sunscreen is an absolute must for runners who train outdoors. Exposure to the sun's harmful UV rays can cause skin cancer. Using a sunscreen with an SPF of 15 or higher can help protect you from this damage. Look for a "sport" product that is long-lasting and sweat-resistant. For long summer runs, you may want to carry a small tube of sunscreen with you to reapply throughout the run.

Equipment

RUNNER'S LUBE

This product is used as a lubricant to avoid chafing under arms, between legs, or anywhere clothing rubs or chafes. Although not as big a problem on shorter-distance runs, on longer runs or when rain or humidity is a factor, chafing can cause pain.

SAFETY WHISTLE

A nonviolent self-protection device recommended for women who run alone, a whistle can be easily attached to a keychain and slipped in the pocket of your running shorts or jacket. Use it to attract attention if you are being attacked or become injured.

WATER BOTTLE AND HOLDER

Great for training in the summer heat, water bottle holders allow you to take fluids with you for a long run. Although the belt around your waist may take some getting used to, the advantages of carrying your own water supply often outweigh any inconvenience or mild discomfort it may cause. Be sure to try carrying a water bottle on a shorter run before taking one out for a long distance.

5

Training

Before You Begin

Before undertaking any physical activity, it's a good idea to schedule an appointment with your physician to get a complete medical checkup. Tell your doctor what you're planning to do, and discuss any medical or health-related concerns you might have. If you are a first-time runner with risk factors such as hypertension, diabetes, asthma, or a family history of coronary artery problems, you should definitely see your doctor before you begin your training. A treadmill stress test can help determine if you have an undiagnosed condition that might put you at greater risk of a heart attack during strenuous exercise.

Choosing a Goal

Once your doctor has cleared you to begin your training program, you can begin in earnest. The first step to starting any marathon training program is selecting a goal to work toward. For most beginning runners—those with little or no recent running experience—the best goal is typically a marathon scheduled at least one year in the future. This will provide enough time for you to build a solid aerobic base before beginning a training program leading up to the event itself. For runners with more experience—those who are already running 15 to 20 miles per week on a regular basis—you can select an event within the next six months. A full training program usually takes around eighteen weeks, so you should continue with your usual weekly running routine leading up to that point.

If you don't already know which event you'd like to train for, refer to the list of major marathons on page 77 of this book. Most major marathons have websites that provide details and descriptions of the event. You can also refer to periodicals such as *Runner's World* or *Running Times* to find lists of smaller local and regional marathons. The choice is truly a personal one. Many first-time runners choose to run in large marathons such as Marine Corps or Chicago, which offer lots of course support and spectators. Others prefer the more personal experience of a smaller regional event, or one that takes place in their hometown. Factors such as the course layout, the weather, and spectator accessibility should all be taken into consideration. One of the best sources of information when choosing a marathon is talking to other runners. Show up at your local running club's weekend run, and ask others there about their marathon experiences. Or, check out some online bulletin boards, which are usually frequented by friendly runners who can help you with your choice. More likely than not you will come away with several good possibilities.

Once you have chosen your event, you can tailor your training schedule to bring you up to that point. Count back from marathon day the number of weeks in your training program, and circle that date on your calendar. This will be the day that your marathon training officially begins.

> **Coach's Tip:** If you are a slower or beginning runner, be sure to check race cutoff times. Many races require you to finish within a certain time. If a race has a 5-hour time limit, you must average about $11\frac{1}{2}$ minutes per mile; a 6-hour time limit requires an average of $13\frac{3}{4}$ minutes per mile. Although training will make you a better runner, do not expect that you will run a faster pace in your first marathon than you are running today.

Building an Aerobic Base: Pretraining

If you are not presently running regularly, it's important for you to first spend at least several months preparing your body to undertake the rigors of a long-distance running program. Following the schedule on the next page, start by combining periods of running and walking, gradually increasing the amount of time you spend running until you are able to run continuously for at least 1 hour. Start out by running very easily until it is uncomfortable for you to continue doing so. Walk for a minute or two until you catch your breath, and then resume easy running. Continue in this fashion until you have completed the required number of minutes.

Coach's Tip: It doesn't matter how fast you run. Speed is not the issue here. For beginners, paces of 10, 11, and even 12 minutes per mile are perfectly acceptable. Most runners improve on these times as they gain fitness, but some runners maintain this slower pace throughout their training. It makes no difference—endurance, not speed, is the key to completing your first marathon.

Throughout this twelve-week schedule, it should become easier for you to spend more time running and less time walking. If by the end of Week 1 you can't run continuously for all sessions, alternate Week 1 and Week 5 until you are able to do so. Depending on your initial level of fitness, you may reach this point by the end of the twelve weeks.

Coach's Tip: During the first few weeks of your training program, don't be tempted to do more than the recommended time even if you feel as if you could. The secret to a successful marathon training program is to start out slowly and gradually build intensity and mileage. Increasing either of these factors too quickly puts you at much greater risk of injury. Try not to increase your mileage by more than 10 to 20 percent per week—you don't want to jeopardize all the progress you're making with one overzealous training session. See pages 49–62 for more information on injury prevention.

Pretraining Program

Week	Mon	Tues	Wed	Thurs	Fri	Sat	Sun
12	Walk/Run 15 min.	Rest	Walk/Run 15 min.	Rest	Walk/Run 15 min.	Rest	Rest
11	Walk/Run 15 min.	Rest	Walk/Run 15 min.	Rest	Walk/Run 15 min.	Rest	Rest
10	Walk/Run 20 min.	Rest	Walk/Run 20 min.	Rest	Walk/Run 20 min.	Rest	Rest
9	Walk/Run 20 min.	Rest	Walk/Run 20 min.	Rest	Walk/Run 20 min.	Rest	Rest
8	Walk/Run 30 min.	Rest	Walk/Run 30 min.	Rest	Walk/Run 30 min.	Rest	Rest
7	Walk/Run 30 min.	Rest	Walk/Run 30 min.	Rest	Walk/Run 30 min.	Rest	Rest
6	Run 20 min.	Rest	Walk/Run 30 min.	Rest	Walk/Run 20 min.	Rest	Walk/Run 40 min.
5	Run 20 min.	Rest	Walk/Run 30 min.	Rest	Walk/Run 20 min.	Rest	Walk/Run 40 min.
4	Run 20 min.	Rest	Walk/Run 30 min.	Rest	Walk/Run 20 min.	Rest	Walk/Run 50 min.
3	Run 20 min.	Rest	Walk/Run 30 min.	Rest	Run 20 min.	Rest	Walk/Run 50 min.
2	Run 20 min.	Rest	Walk/Run 30 min.	Rest	Run 20 min.	Rest	Walk/Run 60 min.
1	Run 20 min.	Rest	Walk/Run 30 min.	Rest	Run 20 min.	Rest	Walk/Run 60 min.

Training for the Marathon

Once you've successfully built up your aerobic base, or if you've already been running regularly for the past several months, you're ready to begin a regular training program. There are a number of marathon training programs in circulation on the Internet and elsewhere. Successful programs generally are designed to gradually build your mileage over the course of your training and then taper in the final two to three weeks. Reproduced below is one of the best-known schedules, the Novice Program developed by Hal Higdon for The La Salle Bank Chicago Marathon; this and other programs are available for free on Higdon's website (www.halhigdon.com) and also in several of his books (see the Resources section on page 79). The program begins eighteen weeks before the marathon with a long run of only 6 miles and a total weekly mileage of 15 miles, and

it culminates three weeks before the event with a 20-mile long run and 40 total miles. This program also contains many of the aspects of successful training programs discussed in this book, including weekly long runs, cross-training*, and rest days.

If you run at a slower pace (11- or 12-minute miles), it may be best to measure your progress by time rather than by distance. For instance, if you were using the Higdon program and averaging 12-minute miles, you would schedule 36 minutes for Week 17's Wednesday run, 48 minutes for Week 16's Wednesday run, and so on. Do not run any longer than scheduled. If you are not able to complete a course in the specified amount of time, walk the remaining distance to recover. This will save excessive wear and tear on your body.

*For guidance on cross-training, see page 58.

Eighteen-Week Training Program

Week	Mon	Tues	Wed	Thurs	Fri	Sat	Sun	Total Mileage
18	Rest	3 miles	3 miles	3 miles	Rest	6 miles	X-train	16
17	Rest	3 miles	3 miles	3 miles	Rest	7 miles	X-train	17
16	Rest	3 miles	4 miles	3 miles	Rest	5 miles	X-train	15
15	Rest	3 miles	4 miles	3 miles	Rest	9 miles	X-train	19
14	Rest	3 miles	5 miles	3 miles	Rest	10 miles	X-train	21
13	Rest	3 miles	5 miles	3 miles	Rest	7 miles	X-train	18
12	Rest	3 miles	6 miles	3 miles	Rest	12 miles	X-train	24
11	Rest	3 miles	6 miles	3 miles	Rest	13 miles	X-train	25
10	Rest	3 miles	7 miles	4 miles	Rest	10 miles	X-train	24
9	Rest	3 miles	7 miles	4 miles	Rest	15 miles	X-train	29
8	Rest	3 miles	8 miles	4 miles	Rest	16 miles	X-train	32
7	Rest	4 miles	8 miles	5 miles	Rest	12 miles	X-train	29
6	Rest	4 miles	9 miles	5 miles	Rest	18 miles	X-train	36
5	Rest	5 miles	9 miles	5 miles	Rest	14 miles	X-train	33
4	Rest	5 miles	10 miles	5 miles	Rest	20 miles	X-train	40
3	Rest	5 miles	8 miles	4 miles	Rest	12 miles	X-train	29
2	Rest	4 miles	6 miles	3 miles	Rest	8 miles	X-train	21
1	Rest	3 miles	4 miles	2 miles	Rest	Rest	RACE	35.2

© Hal Higdon. Used with permission.

Coach's Tip: It's generally OK to do some juggling in order to make your schedule best fit your life. Using the Higdon schedule as an example, if you needed to do your long runs on Sundays in order to meet with a training group, you could simply switch the long run and cross-training days in the schedule. However, do not schedule a run for the day before your long run. Most importantly, maintain the proper number of rest days in your schedule, no matter what. These give your body a chance to recover and prepare for future mileage increases.

The Long Run

The most important part of any successful marathon training program is the long run: the run or runs during your training period that most closely resemble the actual marathon. How long is long enough? For marathoners, 20-mile runs qualify; 30 kilometers (18.6) serves as a round-numbered limit for those using the metric system. The Higdon schedule on page 27 features a 20-mile run as the peak of the program, after which you begin tapering your mileage down until the marathon. The training gains from such a long run are usually not realized for at least three weeks. You spend the early part of your training creating sufficient base mileage to support these long runs. To be safe, runners should have a foundation of several hundred miles of running before attempting a long run.

The pace of these long runs should be 45 seconds to 2 minutes slower than the pace at which you plan to run the marathon. Speed isn't as important as covering the distance and logging the time on your feet. Running too fast risks injury and leaves your muscles fatigued and sore, interfering with quality workouts for days. If you feel as though you are running too slow for your current fitness level, commit to maintaining a slower pace until the last 3 to 5 miles of the run, then pick up the pace through the finish.

It is often advantageous to measure your long runs by time rather than by mileage. The advantage to this approach is that you are not under pressure to run the distance in a specific time, racing the workout against your previous times. A 3-hour run is a 3-hour run, no matter what your pace or the distance you cover. Time-based training can be particularly useful if you train under tough conditions: high altitude, rough trails, inclement weather, or even courses where the exact distance is unknown. Often the best results come from combining the two methods of measurement: One week run for time; the next week, run for distance.

The long run serves a number of different purposes in training your body to complete a marathon. Most significantly, it does the following:

Coach's Tip: Don't be concerned that you won't be able to hold a strong pace through a marathon if you struggle through your long run. A 20-mile training run is not equivalent to the first 20 miles of the marathon. While training, your capabilities are never at 100 percent—far less, actually. Throughout the weeks of training, you are continually breaking down and building up muscle tissue as your body adapts to the longer distances. Tapering and proper nutrition leading up to the marathon allow your body to rest, recover, and store energy so you are fully prepared to run the full distance at 100 percent of your running ability.

- Improves the ability of muscles to store glycogen and to use fat efficiently as fuel (sparing glycogen).
- Improves aerobic and muscular endurance.
- Teaches you to run with relaxed, efficient form for long time periods, despite fatigue.
- Develops patience by forcing you to slow down and pace yourself wisely, just as you must during the marathon.

- Provides a "dress rehearsal" for testing out potential race-day shoes and clothing, energy gels, foods, and fluids.
- Builds psychological endurance and mental toughness by proving that you can indeed cover the distance despite the protests of your mind and body.

Coach's Tip: Be prepared for your long run. If you don't have the luxury of a preplanned course, go out and drive the distance in your car or ride it on your bike the day before, noting mileages at selected points along the course. Also take note of particularly challenging sections of the course and prepare yourself to conquer them. Plan for fluid stops along the way, either by planting them the night before or morning of the run or by running along public trails that have water fountains. In the latter case, carry a water bottle holder with sports drink or make sure that you can purchase some along the course at a convenience store or from a vending machine. See pages 41–43 for more information on the importance of hydration during long runs.

Training in Inclement Weather

Chances are that no matter where you live, at some point you will be forced to train in less-than-ideal conditions. Whether it means running in the cold, rain, heat, or snow, runners who choose to train for a marathon must make the commitment to go out in all sorts of weather. Although you can choose to do your shorter runs inside on a treadmill when conditions are bad, running 16, 18, or 20 miles on a treadmill is simply not practical. Plus, since you have no control over the weather conditions on the day of your event, it's best that you are prepared to run no matter what marathon day might bring.

COLD

Despite the old wives' tale about your lungs freezing, running in the cold is no different than running in any other type of weather. In fact, running in the cold is actually easier on your body, since it's a lot easier for the body to heat itself in the cold than it is to cool itself in the heat. The secret to running comfortably throughout the year is dressing appropriately. In cold weather, this means dressing in layers of the right clothing. You will generate a lot of heat when you run, much more than you expect, so be sure not to overdress. Invest in a good hat, as well as gloves and warm socks. Extremities are usually the first to feel the cold, so if you can keep your hands and feet warm, you're more likely to feel comfortable all over. See page 19 for more tips on dressing to run in cold weather.

Coach's Tip: Don't forget to drink plenty of fluids in the winter. Despite the lower temperatures and humidity, our bodies are just as prone to dehydration during the colder months.

RAIN, SNOW, SLEET, AND ICE

Just like the postal service, marathon runners should be committed to training no matter what form of precipitation falls from the sky. Typically this should not cause any problems, with the exception of freezing rain, which can create dangerous running conditions. If there is ice on the ground, you should consider postponing your run or moving it inside to the treadmill. Snow can create some challenges for road runners in particular, since berms are often left unplowed. Be particularly careful when running on roads in the winter and avoid routes that do not have clear berms. But in rain or sleet, you simply need to dress properly and be conscious of the conditions. Waterproof jackets can provide protection from cold rain and sleet, but in warmer weather, you may just choose to run in your usual clothes and resign yourself to getting soaked. A baseball cap will help to keep rain out of your eyes, leaving you more comfortable and better able to see where you are running. Wear bright colors or a reflective vest when running on dark, rainy days.

Coach's Tip: Be sure to dry your running shoes properly after running in the rain or slush. Remove the inserts and stuff newspaper or paper towels into the toes of the shoes to help them dry more quickly. Don't put running shoes in the dryer, as the high heat will damage the rubber and other shoe materials that provide cushioning.

HEAT

Although you're likely to hear more complaints from runners throughout the winter, running in the heat can actually be much more of a challenge than running in the cold. The ideal running temperature is between 40 and 60 degrees. When running in hot weather, your body has to work overtime to keep cool while supplying oxygen and fuel to the working muscles. Humidity is also a factor. In humid conditions, it's more difficult for the body to cool itself through sweating, since the air is already saturated. The secret to success in heat and humidity is to dress properly, stay hydrated, and adjust your training pace to the conditions of the day.

Clothing should be lightweight and loose-fitting to allow maximum air circulation. Wear light colors that do not absorb heat. Choose fabrics that wick perspiration and will aid in its evaporation. A hat or visor is also a good idea to shade your head and eyes. Sunglasses can help shield your eyes from the glare of the sun.

Hydration is one of the most crucial factors to safe, successful hot-weather training. In the heat and humidity, the body attempts to cool itself by sweating. If these lost fluids are not replaced through drinking, the body cells work inefficiently, sweating decreases, heart rate and body temperature increase, and less blood is available to circulate oxygen and glucose through the body. This is dehydration. In order to prevent dehydration, drink water before, during, and after running, as well as throughout the day. See page 42 for further information on proper hydration.

Another way you can get through training in the heat is to simply adjust your training to accommodate the weather. If you can, it's best to schedule your runs early in the morning or later in the evening in order to avoid the heat of the day. If possible, find a shaded route to run on particularly hot, sunny days. But if you must run in the heat and sun, then you need to slow down and not push yourself as hard. Take walk breaks as needed, especially when it's hot, humid, and hilly. If you run the same routes and courses from week to week, don't try to match the times you are able to run in cooler weather.

High temperatures, humidity, and direct sunlight combined with the heat your body generates when running can cause heat stress, which leads to heat-related illness. The earliest warning signs of heat stress are fatigue, anxiety, irritability, dizziness, or visual impairment. If you recognize and respond to these symptoms, you can avoid serious problems. If you begin to experience any of these symptoms, stop running or slow to a walk. Get out of the sun, and drink water and sports drink. If the symptoms persist or worsen, seek immediate medical attention.

Keeping a Running Log

A running log is your diary, a permanent record of your training as a runner. Over time, it can provide you with valuable information that will help you complete a successful marathon. It documents your progress as a runner, and you can refer to it regularly for guidance. How did I train when I was feeling great? Have I gotten all my long runs in? Did my weight affect the way I ran? Which shoes worked best for me? Your running log can contain the answers to all these questions as well as a summary of the highlights and low points of your training experience.

A running log also can put things in perspective. Sometimes it's difficult to see the successes and failures

of your training while you are experiencing them. But if you look back over the runs from the vantage point of a month or two, you can sometimes notice a pattern. Your log can also help you pinpoint indicators of potential problems. If, for instance, you're experiencing pain in your lower legs, you can look back in your running log and notice that a week ago you ran a particularly hard run in an older pair of shoes

In its most basic form, a running log can be kept in a daily planner, although logs designed specifically for running are available in most bookstores. Each day, write down how far and how long you ran. This is the minimum information that every runner should record. You could also jot down brief comments about the run—the route, weather, or how you felt during the run. Keep track of the miles you cover so you can compile a weekly mileage total. The key is to be consistent. Fill in the information after each run, before you forget the details.

In a more advanced form, your log can also be a diary, which can include a myriad of other information such as the route, time of day, type of workout, average pace, pair of shoes, running partners, and daily resting heart rate and weight. You can also use your log to keep track of race performances and personal records. Your log can be as basic or as detailed as you want it to be. But the more details you choose to include, the more valuable a tool your running log can become.

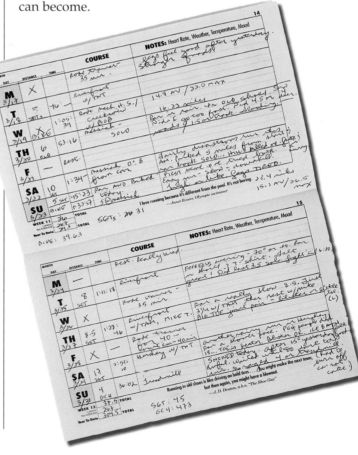

Other Training Strategies

HILL TRAINING

Hill training is the most efficient way to simultaneously build strength and improve aerobic and anaerobic capacity. Running hills, like lifting weights, is a form of resistance training. Hills strengthen the leg muscles to meet the specific demands of running, and by working hard on hills, you force the muscles to overcome the incline and the resistance of gravity. This strengthens the driving muscles—the hamstrings, calves, buttocks, and particularly the quadriceps, which, unfortunately, don't get much work when you run on flat terrain. Fatigued quads can be a problem late in races, especially in the marathon. As a bonus, your ankles will also get a solid workout (from the push-off), as well as your upper arms (from the pumping motion). Hill training will also increase your resistance to fatigue during races, which will help you maintain good running form and a steady pace. Since you have to concentrate on driving the arms, lifting the knees, and pushing off with the feet to get up hills in training, your running form is exaggerated and improved.

You can easily add hill workouts to your regularly scheduled training by substituting one of your shorter weekly runs with a 30- or 40-minute hill workout. Do not add hill running in addition to your scheduled workouts. The best thing to do would be to spend the first third of your training program doing hill training once a week, and then shift to speedwork (see page 33). Make the run the day after a hill workout an easy one, or if possible, do hill workouts the day before a scheduled rest day.

To perform a hill workout, first find a fairly steep hill. The perfect hill has a 4 to 6 percent incline, is fairly consistent from bottom to top, and will take you between 1 and 2 minutes to run. Follow these guidelines:

- Before beginning a hill workout, warm up by running easily for 10 to 15 minutes.
- Stretch before starting your hill repeats, concentrating on your hamstrings and quads.
- Run no more than 4 or 5 hill repeats the first week; you can increase the amount of repeats as your fitness and comfort level improve.
- You want to run at about 85 percent intensity, as if you were running a 10K as hard as you could—fast, but under control. Your intensity and effort should be consistent across each interval.
- Each interval should take the same amount of time to complete. If you slow down over the last couple intervals, you started out too fast. Don't get frustrated if it takes a while to perfect your pacing; it takes practice to push yourself hard enough, but not too hard.

Hill workouts can easily be added to your training program, and can be done alone or with others.

- If there is a flat area at the base of the hill, give yourself a 20- to 30-meter "head start" so that you are not starting on the incline from a dead stop.

31

This eliminates the strain of a standing start on a steep slope.

- Maintain good form running up the hill: head up, arms moving front-to-back, and a slightly exaggerated knee-raise. Shorten your stride so that your leg turnover is the same as it is on flat land.
- Don't stop at the top—run through the "finish line" at the top of the hill. Use the lap timer on your watch to record each uphill/downhill interval. Record these times in your running log.
- Run back down the hill slowly and gently to recover from the uphill and to reduce the impact on your knees and quadriceps. It should take at least twice as long to make your way back to the base of the hill. You should have enough time to at least moderately recover before beginning your next interval.
- After finishing your last interval, cool down by running easily for 10 to 15 minutes. As with any workout, be sure to fully stretch afterward.

Coach's Tip: Hill work can be hard training. It is usually easier and more enjoyable if you can train with a friend who runs at about the same pace as you. Make sure, however, that the two of you do not make the sessions too fast and end up racing to the top of each hill.

STRIDES

Strides, fartleks, accelerations, surges, pickups—there are many names for the same concept: adding brief bursts of speed to your regular running. Strides are 25- to 45-second runs at an accelerated pace that take place during the middle of your training runs. These are not all-out sprints. Simply ramp up the pace so that it's faster than your normal training pace. This should be a fast but sustainable pace, such as the one you would run if you were in a 5K race. After each stride is over, you should recover by running slowly and easily. If you find yourself so out of breath that you can't continue, then you are running your strides too fast and should try moderating the pace.

There are a number of benefits to adding these strides to your regular runs. The main benefit is that speed builds strength. Forcing yourself to run at a faster pace, even for a short period of time, will, with practice, make all your runs faster. Another added benefit is the variety it brings to a workout. Adding strides midrun can break up the monotony of pounding out the miles and give an element of playfulness to your weekly workouts. Running strides with a partner of a similar fitness level can also be fun; each of you can take turns

Maintain good form during hill training.

setting the pace and distance of the stride. This aspect of the workout can also help you learn pacing, since you have no idea how long you will need to maintain the increased level of effort.

When planning to incorporate strides into your own runs, follow these guidelines:

Do:

- Sufficiently warm up before adding a few strides to the run. Run for at least 1 mile before your first stride.
- Incorporate three to six strides into some of your shorter weekly runs.
- Pick out a landmark ahead of you on the road, such as a stop sign, a light pole, or a street corner, rather than striding for a set amount of time. Continue your stride to the landmark instead of staring at your watch.

- Concentrate on form during the stride. Stay relaxed, keep your head up, arms moving front-to-back. Maintain an upright posture with a slight forward lean.
- Return to your normal pace after each stride. It's fine to walk for a bit if you feel winded.
- Record the number of strides you did during the run in your running log.
- Finish your set of strides at least five minutes before the end of your run so that you will have an appropriate amount of time to cool down.

Don't:

- Run strides longer than 45 seconds. At this point in your training, there are no additional fitness benefits to be achieved by extending the duration of each stride.
- Take longer steps to increase your pace. Instead, maintain your stride length and increase your leg turnover to move faster. This is an important concept that will carry forward into future hill and speed work.

- Jam all the strides into one portion of your run. Space them out so that you feel fresh and comfortable before each stride.
- Try to add strides at the same time that you are trying to accomplish another training benefit. For example, don't add strides to your long Saturday run when you are training for endurance.

SPEEDWORK

Although as a first-time marathoner your goal should not be to run the race with an ambitious time in mind, you can still focus some of your training on improving your running speed. Speedwork refers to workouts done on a track or measured course that will help you build not only speed, but also strength that can improve your overall fitness and efficiency as a runner. Speedwork can help you run faster and stronger in three ways:

1. By improving your running form. This will greatly benefit you, especially at the end of your marathon. As you tire, your form deteriorates and you need to concentrate on maintaining it. Because you must run more efficiently to run at a faster speed, speedwork forces you to maintain your form through the entire distance of each repeat.
2. By easing your adaptation to oxygen debt. Running fast increases your ability to breathe and process oxygen through your body.
3. By helping you push through the mental barriers of discomfort and doubt. By doing harder workouts, you start to push yourself and mentally prepare yourself for the rigors of the marathon.

What exactly does speedwork entail? There are a number of different workouts that you can do to prepare for a marathon, but the ones that have the most benefit for marathoners are those that include longer distances—typically 400-, 800-, and 1600-meter repeats.

Speedwork helps to develop your strength and speed.

Basically, what this means is that you will run sets of fast laps around the track (1 lap = 400 meters) interspersed with recovery laps of slow, easy running. Time each repeat (to record in your running log later), and spend at least as much time recovering from each repeat as you spent running it. As you gain strength, gradually increase the distance and number of repeats. You should run the repeats at a pace that is faster than your usual training pace, but not so fast that you cannot finish the workout. It may take a few weeks to get used to maintaining an even pace throughout the course of the workout, but this is one of the goals of speedwork.

You can very easily work speedwork into your regular running schedule just as you integrated hill training. Simply replace one of your shorter weekly runs with a track workout. Do not add the track workout in addition to other weekly runs. With a warmup and cooldown at the beginning and end, the distances are likely to be almost equivalent. The best thing to do would be to concentrate on hillwork once a week (see page 31) for the first third of your training and then move on to speedwork, though you should not do any speedwork the last two weeks before the marathon. Hillwork will allow your body to build the strength and form that will help make speedwork easier.

The chart on the next page demonstrates how to incorporate speedwork into Weeks 12 to 3 of an eighteen-week schedule.

Coach's Tip: When starting a speedwork program, as you begin to increase the intensity of your workouts, you are also increasing the potential for injury. Always be aware of your body, and if you feel anything out of the ordinary, stop your workout immediately. Never start a speedwork program unless you have already established a good base of training.

Follow these guidelines when doing speedwork:
- Warm up sufficiently. Before starting speedwork, run for 10 to 20 minutes to warm up your legs. As you warm up, do several 100-yard pickups at a slowly accelerating speed to get used to going faster.
- After warming up, be sure to stretch completely. Concentrate on the hamstrings, quads, and calves.
- Ease into the workouts. You should finish each workout exhilarated and tired, but not totally exhausted.
- Do speedwork with a partner, if possible. Look for people who run at roughly the same speed as you

do. But remember, each repeat is not a race. Push yourself, but don't hurt yourself.

- Maintain good running form even as you tire at the end of the repeat, but don't sacrifice speed for form.
- Try to run at a consistent pace for all repeats. Don't run the first repeat way too fast and then struggle through the last one, but don't hold back on the first one so that you have too much energy left for the last one. Use the first several weeks to learn your pace.
- Don't overstride. You get faster by having quicker turnover, not a longer stride.
- Fully recover between repeats by easily running.
- Stay hydrated throughout the workout. If there is not a water fountain at the track, take along a water bottle, and drink from it regularly.
- Time yourself on each repeat and record it in your log.
- Cool down by running easy for 10 to 15 minutes and stretch after cooling down.

Speed Training

Week 12	6 × 200m 2 × 400m
Week 11	2 × 400m 2 × 600m 1 × 800m
Week 10	1 × 600m 2 × 800m 1 × 1200m
Week 9	2 × 800m 2 × 1200m
Week 8	2 × 400m 3 × 1200m
Week 7	8 × 200m 1 × 800m
Week 6	2 × 600m 3 × 800m 1 × 1600m
Week 5	2 × 400m 2 × 800m 2 × 1600m
Week 4	3 × 400m 5 × 800m
Week 3	2 × 400m 1 × 800m 3 × 1600m

TRACK ETIQUETTE

- Faster runners have priority on the inside lanes. Run on the inside lanes, but shift to the outside to let people pass you on the inside.
- Be courteous of slower runners or walkers who may be on the track. Say something like "inside" or "on your left" to let them know you are there and wish to pass.
- Move to the outside lanes to cool down.

RACING AS PART OF MARATHON TRAINING

One of the best ways to prepare for the experience of running a marathon is by participating in at least a few races during your training for it. Racing as part of your training has a number of significant benefits.

Most importantly, there is a training benefit: You will generally get a better workout than you do with

You'll improve your training program by adding races at select points in your schedule.

your regular group run. With mile markers and time splits, you will push yourself to run harder and improve your running ability more quickly. You will also gain the psychological benefit of experience.

If you've never participated in a formal race, you may not be aware of the subtleties involved. How do I sign up? How early do I get have to get there? How do I get my bib number and chip, and how do I wear them? Where in the lineup of runners should I start? How fast should I start? You will benefit from learning the answers to these questions through firsthand experience in a race prior to the actual marathon. Racing also provides feedback on how your training is going. If you run a race at the start of your training and one toward the end, you can see how much you improve from race to race. You can also use the information to help you judge the correct pace you should run in a longer race.

Choose a few races to add to your schedule at the beginning of your training program and plan your training around them. Pick a 5K or 10K to insert somewhere into the first five or six weeks of your schedule, and then, if possible, a half-marathon around the halfway point. Run these races as substitutes for your regular long runs. You could simply enter and participate just to gain the experience with a formal race event. Choosing to race them, however, will give you a better idea of the effect race-day adrenaline can have on pace. The decision of whether to really race these events or to run them just for fun is up to you. Either way, racing as a part of your training will provide valuable pre-marathon experience.

Coach's Tip: Some people treat races as just another long run. If you do this you will not be maximizing the race's training benefit. Go into the race with a plan, and decide on a reasonable time goal. Afterwards, reflect on what you did right and what you might have done differently. Keep track of your races. As the actual marathon nears, most of the major running websites have calculators that allow you to enter your time in shorter races and predict your time for the marathon. Although these predictions are only estimates and are sometimes a bit too fast, they can still help you to prepare your pacing for the actual marathon.

Training with Others

As you look over your schedule and the various workouts you'll be doing over the coming months, you may be somewhat daunted by the amount of time and effort you'll be expending on training for the marathon. No doubt, it is a large commitment. One thing that frequently can make the process easier, especially for first-time marathoners, is to train with other people. Training with others provides a great source of motivation and inspiration that you might not get while training on your own. You will also be able to learn from the experience of others and benefit from their knowledge. The emotional support of having a group of people who share the same goal can also make putting in the long miles much easier. Just having some company on long runs makes training with a group worthwhile. A 20-mile run is challenging enough when you have other runners to talk to; running it by yourself can be downright depressing.

Sign up for a program such as the Leukemia and Lymphoma Society's Team in Training or contact your local running club to find out if there is a marathon training group meeting in your area. Don't be intimidated by the thought of training with other people; so many of those training for marathons today are first-timers, and more likely than not they are just as anxious as you are about the rigors of the training program. Don't worry that everyone will be faster than you, either. Large running groups usually have members running at all paces, and chances are that you will not be the slowest person in the group. To find more information on groups such as Team in Training or the Road Runners Clubs of America, see the listings in the Resources section on page 79.

6

Diet and Nutrition

A Runner's Diet

Think of a runner as an automobile. If you don't put gas in the car, it won't run. If you put low-octane fuel in a high-performance car, it will run, but it won't perform at its optimum level. The same is true of your body. As you enter marathon training, your body is becoming a high-performing, efficient machine. You need to give it the proper fuel to enable it to run at its peak level.

Most everyone knows by now the types of foods they should be eating and the types of foods they should not. Fruits, vegetables, whole grains, lean meat, poultry, fish, and low-fat dairy products should form the basis of your diet. You should limit or avoid foods that are high in fat (fried foods and high-fat meats) and high in sugar (sweets and sugary drinks). But as a runner, you should fine-tune your daily diet even more. Not only should you concentrate on eating the right kinds of foods, but you also should try to eat the right amounts of them. As a runner, your diet should be structured to provide 60 to 70 percent of your daily caloric intake from carbohydrates, 10 to 15 percent from protein, and 20 to 25 percent from fat.

Why so many carbohydrates? The fuel for powering your muscles while running is glycogen. Glycogen is created when the body breaks down carbohydrates into simple sugars to be stored in the body. About 78 percent of this glycogen is stored in your muscles, 18 percent in the liver, and the rest in your bloodstream. When at rest, the body has plenty of oxygen, and it burns fat in conjunction with the glycogen. But when you run, oxygen is less available, and the body, looking for a better source of fast fuel, turns to glycogen. The more carbohydrates you consume as you train, the more glycogen you are able to store. An untrained muscle can store 13 grams of glycogen for each kilogram of muscle. With proper training, this amount rises to 32 grams. The best sources of carbohydrates for runners are the wholesome complex carbohydrates found in foods such as pasta and rice. Some sources of simple carbohydrates are also good.

Although the focus for runners should definitely be carbohydrates, protein and fat are also essential parts of a runner's diet. Make sure that you eat a small serving of lean meat, eggs, or low-fat dairy products at least twice per day. Soy products can also provide a healthy source of protein for both vegetarians and nonvegetarians. You probably won't have to try as hard to get fat in your diet, but you should be conscious of which kind of fat you should be eating. Limit saturated fats, as well as fried foods that are cooked in oils containing saturated fats. Unsaturated fats are a much better choice.

Running and Weight Control

Some first-time runners have the misconception that because they run, they can eat whatever they want and not worry about gaining weight. Unfortunately, this is not the case. Although running does provide an excellent means of weight control, it does not give you a free ticket to eat as much of whatever you want.

Despite the preponderance of diets touting high-protein or low-fat secrets to weight loss, what it basically comes down to is simple mathematics. You must figure out exactly how many calories your body needs to maintain itself each day and not consume in excess of that amount. This is where running comes in: since you will be burning extra calories through exercise, you can actually eat a few more calories per day and still break even. But you still have to make sure you aren't consuming too much. Here's how:

1. The first step in figuring this out is to determine exactly how many calories you consume per day. The best way to do this is to write everything down. Include each meal and snack as well as all beverages you consume. Then refer to a calorie calculator and add it all up.
2. The next step in figuring out how many calories you need is to determine your Basal Metabolic Rate (BMR). This is the actual number of calories your body requires to keep itself functioning. (There are a number of free BMR calculators

Nutrition Basics

Foods are broken down into three main categories: carbohydrates, proteins, and fats. Carbohydrates provide the basic fuel for your body to function. The body converts carbohydrates into glucose, also known as blood sugar. The extra glucose that the body does not immediately need is stored in the body as glycogen. But the body's capacity to store glycogen is limited; any extra carbohydrates not used immediately for fueling the body are stored as fat. There are two types of carbohydrates: complex and simple. Complex carbohydrates are broken down more slowly in the body and include starches like bread, pasta, rice, and starchy vegetables such as potatoes and corn. Simple carbohydrates are broken down more quickly in the body and include all the sugars: fructose (in fruit), lactose (in milk), and sucrose (table sugar), as well as honey, corn syrup, and high fructose corn syrup. Both simple and complex carbohydrates contain 4 calories per gram.

Protein helps the body build and maintain muscle and body tissue. As with carbohydrates, the body stores any protein it does not use as fat. Although there is only one type of protein, some of it is considered to be "lean" because it has a lower fat content than other types. Examples of lean protein include fish, chicken, turkey, lean meats, and low-fat dairy and soy products. Protein also has 4 calories per gram.

Dietary fat is necessary to insulate the body from cold, to protect internal organs, and to maintain skin and hair. The body also stores extra energy by converting excess carbohydrates and protein to fat. There are two types of fats: saturated fats, such as lard, butter, margarine, and vegetable shortening (mainly fats that are solid at room temperature); and unsaturated fats, such as olive oil, vegetable oil, and corn oil (mainly fats that are liquid at room temperature). The so-called "trans fats" are unsaturated fats such as corn oil that are put through a chemical process known as hydrogenization to make them more solid at room temperature. Trans fats have recently become controversial, as several studies have shown that they may be more damaging to health than saturated fats. In addition to avoiding trans fats, diets lower in saturated fats are recommended. All fats contain 9 calories per gram.

available on the Internet; one is at www.global-fitness.com under "Free Fitness Tools.")

3. The final step is figuring out how many calories you burn per day doing all the various activities in your day—everything from basic housework to gardening to the running and cross-training you do for marathon training. (The free BMR calculator also includes a helpful estimator for calorie expenditure.)

Once you have all this information, you can do the following calculation:

> **Calories consumed**
> **− calories required (BMR)**
> **− calories expended**
>
> **= caloric deficit or caloric surplus**

If the number you come up with is positive, that means after a repeated period of surpluses, you will gain weight. If the number is negative, that means after an extended period of deficits, you will lose weight. If the number is around 0, you will maintain your present weight. Keep in mind that it takes a deficit of 3500 calories to lose 1 pound of excess fat.

Here's an example. A 155-pound woman preparing to train for her first marathon wants to lose some weight before the race. She figures out that she consumes 2200 calories per day and that her BMR is approximately 1500 calories. Including her training (1 hour of running at a 12-minute-per-mile pace, which burns 560 calories), her daily activities burn 1000 calories. Here's how she would figure it out:

> **2200 calories consumed**
> **− 1500 calories required (BMR)**
> **− 1000 calories expended**
>
> **= 300 calorie deficit**

Maintaining a caloric deficit of 300 calories per day, it would take this woman approximately twelve days to lose 1 pound. If she wants to lose a total of 10 pounds, that will take four months. If she wants to reduce the time by half, losing 10 pounds in two months, she can either reduce the number of calories she takes in or increase her activity level to burn more calories.

Keep in mind that experts recommend that 1 to 2 pounds per week is a safe rate to take off weight, so don't reduce your caloric intake too drastically. Since you will be increasing your activity level as you build your training anyhow, you may notice that you are losing weight more quickly without even trying. Just be sure that you are meeting your caloric requirements without overeating.

Eating to Run

PRERUN EATING

Part of your training involves figuring out how your eating affects your running. Although it's less important on days when you're running shorter distances, there is no doubt that what you eat before a long run—or whether you eat at all—will affect how you feel and how well you perform. Some people can eat a full meal and then go right out and run shortly afterward. Other runners experience gastrointestinal problems if they try to run shortly after eating a meal and opt for something small, such as a glass of orange juice or a sports bar, instead. You need to experiment to see what works best for you.

If you do eat before a long run, it should be a meal high in carbohydrates, low in fat, and with moderate protein content. Oatmeal and a banana makes the perfect breakfast for some runners. Others prefer a bagel with peanut butter. Whatever you choose, portions should be moderate. You should also take extra fluids with the meal. Water or a sports drink are two obvious choices. To avoid sugar highs (and crashes), it is best to avoid sugars in the 45 minutes before running.

Coach's Tip: Even on the days when you are running shorter distances, you will probably find that eating certain foods right before you run causes problems. Foods that are high in fat or fiber are usually best avoided. Some runners also have trouble with dairy products. The best thing to do is to make a note of which foods adversely affect you during your training, and avoid them in the future.

POSTRUN REFUELING

When you run, your body uses up its stored glycogen. After your run, your job is to replace that glycogen by consuming carbohydrates. In the first half hour to an hour after you finish running, your body is best conditioned to manage this task, so you should try to eat and drink at least 300 calories' worth of carbohydrates in that window of time. Some good recovery food and drinks include apple juice, bagels, bananas, and sports drinks. You should then follow up this postrun snack with a full meal sometime within the next few hours in order to top off your glycogen stores.

Research is beginning to show that protein can also aid postrun recovery by giving the body the raw materials to help rebuild damaged muscle tissue. A small amount of protein paired with carbohydrates—such as in yogurt—might be a good choice. Several bars also include protein as well as carbohydrates and can be easily carried or kept in the car. Make sure that your postrun meal also includes enough protein.

Eating and Drinking on the Run

The body stores enough glycogen to allow you to run for 90 minutes to 2 hours without any additional sources of carbohydrates. As you increase the amount of time you spend on your training runs, as well as when you run the marathon, you will need to resupply your body with fuel. This fuel on-the-go can come from three sources: solid food, sports drinks, and/or energy gels. Solid food is least often used by runners when running because it takes a lot longer to digest and has a higher likelihood of upsetting the stomach. The other two sources have become increasingly popular over the past few years, and most runners take advantage of one or both of them to get through their long training runs as well as the marathon itself.

Sports drinks such as Gatorade, All Sport, Powerade, and Ultima are mixtures of sugars and water. Most also include electrolytes, such as sodium and potassium, and vitamins. They typically range between 6 and 12 percent carbohydrates and are useful for replenishing lost fluids and replacing carbohydrates. They also help the body replace the electrolytes lost through sweat and prevent dehydration. It's important to consume sports drinks in addition to water, especially during the marathon, in order to avoid a dangerous condition known as hyponatremia, in which excess water consumption endangers the body's electrolyte balance. Alternate sips of water and sports drink on

Sports drinks help to restore fluids and electrolytes.

Energy gels provide concentrated carbohydrates.

the course can easily prevent this potentially life-threatening condition.

Energy gels are a relatively new addition to the marathoning scene. Product names include Gu, PowerGel, Carb-Boom, and Clif Shots. These gels are concentrated mixtures of pure carbohydrates. They are more easily digested than solid food and easier to carry than sports drinks. Two words of caution on the use of energy gels: First of all, training teaches your body to adapt by storing more glycogen to use during a run. If, during your training, you start to use energy gels too early in your runs, you will fool your body into thinking it does not need to make the physiological changes required to store more fuel. Then when you do need the extra glycogen, it won't be there. Second, since gels are pure carbohydrates, that means they are pure sugar. Once you start using gels during a run, you will need to use them every 30 to 45 minutes or so to avoid a sugar crash.

When should you start using gels on a run? You should not use gels at all for runs less than 90 minutes in duration. Your body will have enough stored carbohydrates to get you through these shorter runs without any supplementation. For runs longer than 90 minutes, you should experiment with a few different scenarios to see which works best. Some people take a gel after 45 minutes of running and then every 30 to 45 minutes thereafter. Others prefer to wait until 90 minutes or so into the run and then take one. See which method works best for you, but don't forget to take along enough gels to allow you to take one every 30 to 45 minutes in order to avoid a sugar crash. To aid in digestion, be sure to drink plenty of water with each gel.

Coach's Tip: Check the event website or contact the race director to find out which sports drink and/or energy gel your marathon will have on the course. If possible, try to use these products during your training runs. This will familiarize you with their qualities and give you a good indication of how they affect your body. If you find that you can't tolerate either the drink or the gel, you will need to arrange to provide your own by carrying them with you. For fluids, you can wear a water bottle holder and replenish your supply by giving extra bottles to your friends and family to give you at predetermined points on the course. Gels can easily be pinned to shorts or carried in your pockets.

Hydration

To hydrate means to replace your body's lost fluids. Water is the body's most important nutrient. We are made up of more than 70 percent water, and our bodies will not function properly if water lost through exercise is not replenished. The chemical process of breaking down carbohydrates for fuel requires water, so proper fluid intake is even more important when you run. The following are some general guidelines on hydration during your training. See chapter 10 for tips on hydration during the marathon itself.

1. Keep adequately hydrated every day, not just on days that you are running. The most common advice is to drink at least eight 8-ounce glasses of water every day. Keep a water bottle on your desk at work and a pitcher of cold water in the refrigerator at home. You know that you are well hydrated if your urine is clear or a very light yellow.
2. Coffee, tea, and alcohol act as diuretics and thus increase water loss from the body. As you consume them, your need to replace water also increases. Don't drink alcohol the day before a long run or strenuous exercise and for at least two days before the marathon. If it's part of your

normal breakfast routine, a cup of coffee or tea before a race or long run is fine.

3. Drink 12 to 16 ounces of water before you run. You may need to find a bathroom somewhere on the course, but that is definitely preferable to running while dehydrated. When racing, drink up to about 2 hours before the start of the race, and then stop. This will allow the excess fluids to pass through your system before the race. Then, about 15 minutes before the starting gun, drink 8 to 12 ounces more.

4. Don't wait until you're thirsty to drink during a long run. You should consume 4 to 8 ounces of fluid every 15 to 20 minutes. Plan courses that include water fountains (churches, fire stations, some grocery stores, and parks are good bets) or convenience stores where you can buy water or carry water with you. A water bottle belt (pictured at right) is a good investment if you can become accustomed to it.

5. After the run, drink plenty of fluids. Refuel your body with water and sports drink in the first half hour after a strenuous workout. This is when your muscles are most receptive to water and nutrients.

7

Women's Running

History of Women Marathoners

In 2002, 40 percent of the 450,000 marathon finishers were female. That's 180,000 women who crossed the finish line with their fellow male runners. Perhaps this number is not as surprising to those of us who have grown up with the landmark 1972 Title IX legislation, which guaranteed equal participation in sports for girls in federally funded schools, in place. But to put things in perspective, just eight years after Title IX took effect, in 1980, women accounted for only 10.5 percent of the 120,000 total marathon finishers, or just 12,600 women. In a little over twenty years, women's participation in marathoning has quadrupled.*

*Statistics from the USA Track & Field Road Running Information Center, www.runningusa.org.

Women runners have not always been so welcome. An infamous story from the 1967 Boston Marathon illustrates how far women have come. After Roberta Gibb's unofficial running of the prestigious event the year before, Kathrine Switzer applied for the race in 1967 under the name "K. V. Switzer" and was issued an official bib number. When a race official realized that a women was running the marathon with a number, he attempted to physically remove her from the course at Mile 4. Her fellow runners tackled the official, allowing Switzer to continue running and finish the race. Four years later, the Amateur Athletics Union (AAU) officially voted to allow women to participate in its sanctioned events, and in 1972, eight women started and finished the Boston Marathon. Nina Kuscsik, was the

When Kathrine Switzer entered the 1967 Boston Marathon, race officials attempted to pull her from the course. Switzer's fellow runners moved in to protect her and succeeded in removing official Jack Semple from the race.

Running through Pregnancy

The American College of Obstetricians and Gynecologists (ACOG) has recently revised its recommendations to state that pregnant women should "engage in 30 minutes or more of moderate exercise on most, if not all, days of the week." But moderation is the key. And since marathon training and moderation typically do not go hand in hand (20-mile-long runs are anything but "moderate"), if you are pregnant right now or are planning to get pregnant in the months ahead, you should probably put your marathon training plans on hold. You can safely return to your prepregnancy running routine following the birth of your baby, but do so gradually, and with the guidance of your gynecologist or obstetrician. For more details on running through pregnancy, visit the ACOG website at www.acog.org and request Patient Education Pamphlet AP119, "Exercise during Pregnancy."

---

first to cross the line with a time of 3:10:26. Other large national marathons followed suit in the 1970s, but it was not until 1984 that the marathon was offered to women as an Olympic sport. In that year, American Joan Benoit Samuelson won in Los Angeles with a time of 2:24:52. Samuelson's Olympic record stood until 2000 when Japanese marathoner Naoko Takahashi finished at Sydney in 2:23:14.

Women's times have continued to improve over the years that they have been running. The first woman to break the 3-hour barrier in a marathon was Adreienne Beames of Australia, who ran a 2:46:30 in 1971. By 1985, the women's world record had dropped to 2:21:06, an amazing feat by Norwegian Ingrid Kristiansen in London. Her record stood for almost fifteen years, until 1998, when Kenyan Tegla Loroupe beat it by 19 seconds at the Rotterdam Marathon with a time of 2:20:47. Three years later, Japanese runner and Olympic marathon record holder Naoko Takahashi broke the 2:20 barrier with a time of 2:19:46 at the Berlin Marathon. The current women's world record as of the time of this writing is Briton Paula Radcliffe's amazing 2:15:25 performance in the 2003 London Marathon, beating her previous world record of 2:17:18 by nearly 2 minutes. This brings women within $10^1/_2$ minutes of the current men's world record time of 2:04:55, set by Kenyan Paul Tergat in Berlin in 2003.

Women's Bodies and Marathon Training

One of the obstacles the early women marathoners had to overcome was the misconception that women's bodies were not intended to be put through such rigors as long-distance marathon training. For many years, women were thought to be incapable of running more than short distances, and the sight of women in the 1970s competing in long-distance events alongside men was seen as nothing less than shocking. While it is a biological fact that men's bodies on average have greater muscle mass, stronger bones, and a greater aerobic capacity, there is no physical limitation caused by gender differences that prevents women from competing alongside men. But these physical differences are likely to prevent women from ever completely eliminating the disparity between the men's and women's world record times for the marathon. Noting the progress women have made in just the past thirty years or so, however, it is conceivable that the gap will continue to narrow.

One of the main differences between men's and women's bodies is in the levels of body fat each contains. The average healthy American woman has a body fat percentage of roughly 25 to 30 percent, compared with a healthy American man's 15 to 20 percent. These extra percentage points mean that men, on average, have more muscle mass than women and can therefore more effectively burn carbohydrates. Women's body fat is typically tied to the physiological requirements of childbearing and breast feeding, both of which rely on stored body fat. Even women who are no longer of childbearing age or do not have children typically maintain higher body fat percentages.

Women's Nutrition

Women's nutritional needs are different from men's. And for the woman runner, it is even more important to recognize the difference. Because women are usually smaller than men, and therefore require fewer calories to maintain their bodies, it is even more important for women to choose the right foods to provide the nutrition they need. Avoid junk food that adds calories and provides no nutritional value, and aim to eat fruits, grains, and vegetables to supply your caloric needs.

One nutritional advantage women have over men is that women runners burn a higher ratio of fat to carbohydrates than do men. Because women draw more efficiently from their fat stores, their reserves of stored carbohydrates (or glycogen) last longer. This may explain why women perform better than most men in ultramarathon (100 miles or longer) competitions. But like men, women still need to concentrate on topping up their glycogen stores in the week leading up to the marathon (see page 68 for more details on prerace nutrition).

Just because you are loading up on carbohydrates, however, does not mean that you can ignore protein. Runners—both men and women—need more protein than an average sedentary person in order to maintain muscle mass. Low-fat choices, such as fish or chicken, should provide most of your protein needs. Soy is another excellent choice, as are nuts and beans. Low-fat dairy products also provide the added benefit of bone-increasing calcium. Protein also aids in repairing muscle damage, so it's especially important to include enough in your diet in the days following a tough training run or race.

One final nutritional issue women should pay particular attention to is iron. Because women lose iron each month through their menstrual cycles, it is essential for women to get enough iron through their diet in order to avoid a deficiency. Red meat offers the best source for iron, but it is also available in beans, raisins, green leafy vegetables, and some fortified breakfast cereals. Eaten in conjunction with vitamin C–rich foods such as oranges and strawberries, which aid in iron absorption, a diet rich in these foods can provide for a woman's iron needs without requiring a dietary supplement. But if, as you begin your training, you experience excessive fatigue or an intolerance to cold temperatures, see your doctor for an iron assessment to determine if you might be suffering from iron-deficient anemia.

Women's Safety Issues

Although every runner should be conscious of safety when running, women should be particularly vigilant, especially when running alone. A recent *Runner's World* online poll found that most runners don't take this advice to heart. Less than 50 percent wear reflective clothing when running at night; only 23 percent have taken a self-defense class; and just 6 percent always run with a partner. Although women should not allow safety concerns to keep them off the roads, there are several things they can do to make themselves safer.

The following "Tips for Running Safety" from the Road Runners Club of America (RRCA) apply to all runners, but should be particularly important for women:

1. Don't wear headsets. Use your ears to be aware of your surroundings. Using headphones, you lose the use of an important sense: your hearing.
2. Always stay alert and aware of what's going on around you. The more aware you are, the less vulnerable you are.
3. Carry a cell phone or change for a phone call. Know the locations of call boxes and telephones along your regular route.
4. Trust your intuition about a person or an area. React on your intuition and avoid a person or situation if you're unsure. If something tells you a situation is not "right," it isn't.
5. Alter or vary your running route pattern; run in familiar areas if possible. In unfamiliar areas, such as while traveling, contact a local RRCA club or running store. Know where open businesses or stores are located.
6. Run with a partner. Run with a dog.
7. Write down or leave word of the direction of your run. Tell friends and family of your favorite running routes.
8. Avoid unpopulated areas, deserted streets, and overgrown trails. Especially avoid unlit areas, especially at night. Run clear of parked cars or bushes.
9. Carry identification or write your name, phone number, and blood type on the inside sole of your running shoe. Include any medical information. Don't wear jewelry.
10. Ignore verbal harassment. Use discretion in acknowledging strangers. Look directly at others and be observant, but keep your distance and keep moving.
11. Run against traffic so you can observe approaching automobiles.
12. Wear reflective material if you must run before dawn or after dark.
13. Practice memorizing license tags or identifying characteristics of strangers.
14. Carry a noisemaker and/or OC (pepper) spray. Get training in self-defense and the use of pepper spray.
15. Call police immediately if something happens to you or someone else, or you notice anyone out of the ordinary. It is important to report incidents immediately.

In addition to these things that you can do while running, you can also prepare yourself to avert a potential attack by taking a self-defense class. Many local YMCAs, colleges, and universities offer self-defense classes especially designed for women. These courses often spend as much time on teaching women how to reduce the risk of being attacked as they do teaching how to defend themselves against an attacker. Once a woman has gained the assurance of knowing that she can deal with a potentially dangerous situation, she gains the confidence to run more assertively. Body language can mean the difference between being selected as a target and being left alone.

8

Injury Prevention

Getting to the Starting Line

You can't finish a marathon if you never make it to the starting line. If you can make it to the starting line healthy and uninjured, there is a very good chance that you will make it to the finish line. Paradoxically, it is not being underprepared that keeps many beginners from making it to the starting line. Rather, it is typically injuries caused by overtraining that prevent first-time marathoners from participating in their intended event. In their overzealous excitement, beginning runners tend to run too much rather than too little and fail to listen to their bodies when injuries start to crop up. The information in this chapter will provide several different strategies for avoiding injuries before they occur. In addition to aspects of your regular training that help prevent injury, the addition of stretching, cross-training, and weight training can help improve your resistance to potential injuries.

Training to Avoid Injury

Most running injuries are not caused by sudden impact, such as the wrenching of a knee on the basketball court, but by overdoing certain stresses, causing what are known as overuse injuries. The repetitive motion of running—the continuous pounding of feet and legs against pavement—raises the risk of biomechanical breakdown. Calf muscles can hurt, Achilles tendons can swell, knee joints can ache. Newer runners are particularly susceptible to these types of injuries, because they are so eager to progress in the sport that they think putting in longer or harder miles will help them improve faster. Unfortunately, as many new runners learn the hard way, this is not the case.

THE DANGERS OF OVERTRAINING

You can easily avoid falling into the overtraining trap by sticking to an established training schedule, such as the Higdon schedule reproduced on page 27. Beginner's programs such as that one are designed to keep you

within as safe zone of total mileage and to provide a steady, gradual increase in mileage from week to week. As a general rule, you should not increase your weekly mileage by more than 10 to 20 percent in any given week.

Most good marathon training programs also include what is known as a "step-back week"—a week to back off the amount of mileage after two successive weeks of increase. These step-back weeks become more and more important as your total mileage increases toward the peak of your training program. The respite that is provided is both mentally and physically rejuvenating and should be maintained throughout your training program.

Coach's Tip: If you miss a run during the week because of a scheduling conflict, *do not* try to make up the mileage for the week by tacking it on to another run. This is how people end up getting injured. Just let that day go and consider it an unscheduled rest day. In the long term, a few of these days here and there will not make a difference. Missing long runs, however, is a more serious complication and requires an adjustment to your training schedule.

WEARING PROPER SHOES

Before any beginning runner undertakes a marathon training program, it is essential to invest in a quality pair of running shoes. The white "sneakers" you've been wearing to aerobics classes for the past few years simply will not hold up to the rigors of long-distance running. See pages 15–17 for more information on buying the right running shoe.

GETTING ENOUGH SLEEP

Although individuals' personal sleep requirements vary, in general most active adults should get 8 to 9 hours of sleep per night. One of the fringe benefits of an active lifestyle is that you sleep much more soundly and should awake feeling more rested. Sleep is the time your body takes to repair the damage you do to it during the course of training. Muscles are strengthened, joints can heal, and the immune system can recharge itself. As you progress through your training program you should be increasingly aware of the need to get plenty of sleep.

RUNNING ON SOFTER SURFACES

Running on softer surfaces is one easy way to give your body a break from the repetitive stress of running on pavement. The constant pounding against concrete (the worst) and asphalt (not much better) can begin to take a toll on your joints. Switching a long run to a well-packed dirt trail can make all the difference in how you feel the next day. Some veteran runners have forgone paved surfaces entirely, choosing to do all their running on softer surfaces to save their joints.

Many of the "Rails to Trails" areas are perfect for such long runs. They are typically well shaded and flat and offer a nice change of pace from road running. If you are more adventurous, many areas have trail networks in local and state parks that are good for running. These trails are usually rockier and more hilly than rail-bed conversions and should be run at a slower, more cautious pace than flat trails. Although trail running shoes are not absolutely necessary, their stiffer construction and better traction can help you negotiate the trail's surface better than standard running shoes.

Opting for softer surfaces on occasion will ease the stress on your body.

One of the most important things you can do to prevent injury is to incorporate a regular stretching program into your training. Your program does not have to be overly complex or time-consuming. But stretching for just 10 minutes per day at least five times per week can produce enormous benefits. In addition to staving off potential injuries, you will also gain greater flexibility and range of motion, which will improve your overall level of fitness and athletic performance.

WHEN TO STRETCH

Should you stretch before or after a run? Or both? There are conflicting answers to this question. Some experts believe that the most benefit is gained from stretching before a long run, after a 5- to 10-minute warmup. Others feel that the best time to stretch is following a run, once the muscles have done their work. At a minimum, you should always stretch after you complete a run. Does that mean that as soon as you take your last step you should begin stretching? Not necessarily. Most people stretch after they have cooled down and had a chance to get something to drink. This is usually a good time, because your muscles will still be warm but you won't be tempted to rush through your stretching because you are hot or thirsty. Other runners like to stretch before they run. If you do a short warmup before stretching, you may benefit from a prerun stretch. Prerun stretching is particularly important if you have been experiencing tightness in certain areas such as your hamstrings, Achilles tendon, or iliotibial (IT) band.

Whether you stretch before or after your run, there are a few general rules that you should observe when stretching:

- Never stretch a cold muscle. Always do something first to warm up your muscles, such as light exercise, or taking a hot shower. Never hop out of bed in the morning and start a hard stretching exercise.
- Stretch slowly and gradually. Never stretch a muscle to the point that the stretch hurts. You should feel the stretch, but not to the point of pain.
- Repeat each stretch three and five times. Hold each stretch for 20 to 30 seconds. After 30 seconds, the benefits of stretching begin to greatly diminish.
- Don't bounce. One tendency for people new to stretching is to bob up and down, trying to get a greater stretch. This tremendously increases your chance of pulling and injuring a muscle.
- Stretch regularly. You can stretch anywhere—in the shower, or while watching TV or reading the paper. Just do it at least five times a week. Doing it every day as part of your regular routine is even better. Ten minutes a day may be sufficient.
- Relax when you stretch. Breathing normally allows oxygen to get to the muscles and increases the benefits of stretching.

1. Upper Calf Stretch

Facing a wall or tree, keep your heel on the ground and your back leg straight. Lean into the wall or tree until you feel a stretch in your calf muscle. When done with the back leg straight, this stretch targets the gastrocnemius, or upper calf muscle.

2. Lower Calf Stretch

As for the previous stretch, face a wall or tree and lean inward, keeping the heel on the ground. But for this stretch, bend the back leg until you feel a stretch in your calf. When done with the back leg bent, this stretch targets the soleus, or lower calf muscle.

3. Quadriceps Stretch

Holding onto a tree, car, or railing for balance, pull the heel of one leg toward your buttock. Make sure your knee is pointing straight down. Keep the knee of your other leg relaxed. Pull until you feel a stretch in the front of your thigh.

4. Hip Flexor Stretch

With one leg forward and the other leg back, keeping the back straight, bend at the knee and dip the hips downward until you feel a stretch in the front of the hip.

Injury Prevention

5. Adductor Stretch

Stand with legs spread apart and bend one knee. Shift your weight toward the bent knee to stretch the adductors of the straight leg.

6. Abductor (Iliotibial Band) Stretch

Leaning against a tree or wall for support, cross your ankles and press the inside leg against the outside leg to stretch the abductors of the outside leg.

Injury Prevention

54

7. Groin Stretch

Sitting with the back straight, bring the soles of your shoes together and bend forward from your hips. Use your elbows to push your knees downward until you feel a stretch in the groin area.

8. Hamstring Stretch

With legs spread apart as far as comfortable, bend forward at the waist and reach out with your arms as far as possible until you feel a stretch in the back of your legs.

Injury Prevention

9. Hamstring Stretch

With the right leg extended and the left leg bent with foot toward crotch, lean forward from the hips and reach toward your right foot until you feel a stretch in the back of your leg.

10. Hamstring Stretch (assisted)

Lying on your back, have a partner place one hand on your ankle and another just above your knee and gently pull your extended leg backward until you feel a stretch in the back of your leg.

11. Piriformis Stretch

Lying down flat on your back with one leg extended and the other knee slightly bent, pull the knee over the extended leg until you feel a stretch in your outer hip.

12. Back Extension Stretch

Lying face down with your arms in front of you, push your torso up off the ground, arching your back until you feel a stretch in the lower back.

Injury Prevention

Cross-training is, simply, the use of one or more sports or activities other than running to enhance your overall fitness level. The cross-training day is a key part of many training schedules and should be viewed as an easy day. Thus, any activity you engage in should not be overly taxing or strenuous. If you're feeling at all run-down and tired, turn the cross-training day into a rest day.

Cross-training can have many benefits to runners, including the following:

- Enhancing the quality of your training.
- Improving overall body strength and endurance.
- Reducing your risk of injury.
- Adding variety to your workout schedule.
- Maintaining fitness through periods of minor injuries.

Cross-training can be broken down into three types of activities: complementary, replacement, and strength training.

COMPLEMENTARY CROSS-TRAINING
Complementary activities primarily work muscle groups that running does not. Examples include swimming, cross-country skiing (or ski machine), aerobics, walking, or rowing machine. Any exercise or sport that is low-impact, maintains an elevated heart rate (60 to 70 percent of maximum), and works on the upper body (arms, shoulders, chest, back, abdomen) is a great choice. A developed upper body helps minimize fatigue in your arms and shoulders, improve your running economy when you start to tire, and make you a stronger hill runner.

REPLACEMENT CROSS-TRAINING
Replacement activities are similar to running but typically should be lower-impact and less strenuous. Examples include stair climbing, cycling, or elliptical trainer. Replacement sports are great if you can't run because of bad weather, minor aches and pains, or travel. Workouts including these activities are great low-impact substitutes for your shorter runs. As with complementary cross-training, maintain an elevated (training zone) heart rate for solid aerobic conditioning.

STRENGTH TRAINING
A third classification of cross-training is strength training. Training with weights also provides another main strategy to help ward off running-related injuries. When some people think of strength training, they think of bodybuilders with bulging muscles. But for runners, this is not the kind of strength training you will benefit from. You will not be training to add body mass—you don't need to be carrying around this excess weight when you run. But since when you run, you are using muscles, it stands to reason that if you strengthen those muscles, you can run better. This is true not only of your legs but also of your abdominal muscles and your upper body. By keeping these core muscles strong, you will tire less easily and be able to maintain a faster pace for a longer period of time.

Strength training adds other benefits to your running and your overall health:

- Prevents injuries. Strong muscles help support the joints. A large number of injuries occur in the tendons and ligaments around the joints. By strengthening your muscles, you can decrease the impact of pounding on the joints.
- Improves running and racing form. With increased strength, you can run more efficiently with less muscle fatigue and maintain your form for a longer period of time.
- Counteracts the natural effects of aging. As we age, we naturally lose muscle mass. Strength training can help slow this loss.
- Controls your weight. A pound of muscle burns 30 to 50 calories a day to maintain itself while at rest. A pound of fat burns only 2 calories. Adding muscle helps control your weight without reducing your caloric intake.

How to Strength Train
As a runner, you should strength train by lifting lighter weights in repetitive sets. A repetition (rep) is lifting the same weight multiple times. Initially, you should do one repetitive set (or maybe two) of eight to twelve lifts. Over the course of your training, you can gradually increase this to three reps. During the period that you are training, do not strength train more than two days per week; in the off-season when you are not training, you may increase this to three days per week.

A personal trainer at your local gym can help you develop a specific weight-training program that is best tailored to suit your needs, but in general, here are the main muscle groups that runners should target:

- Abdominal muscles. The source of a great deal of your running strength comes from the center of your body. By strengthening this area, you can improve your ability to run stronger and faster for longer periods of time.
- Upper body. By strengthening the shoulders, upper chest, and upper back, you will improve your running form and increase your efficiency.
- Legs and hips. Running already helps build strong quads. By strengthening the backs of your legs (hamstrings), you will help prevent injuries by creating a better-balanced muscle group. Working calf muscles and shins can also help prevent common injuries.

Coach's Tip: As you reach the peak of your marathon training program and enter your taper, you should stop or very significantly reduce strength training to allow your body to dedicate its resources to preparing for the marathon. Throughout your training, it's also best to avoid weight-training legwork on days before races, speedwork, or long runs. Never do back-to-back days of strength training. Allow at least one day of rest between weight-training workouts to give your muscles time to heal from the previous session. This is how you build muscular strength.

Cycling is one of several possible cross-training activities.

No matter how carefully you observe the above strategies for avoiding injuries, if you continue to run longer distances, at some point in your running career an injury is likely to occur. Recognizing the early symptoms of an injury right away and treating it properly will help minimize its impact and restore you to health in a shorter period of time.

COMMON RUNNING INJURIES

Most running injuries are repetitive stress injuries caused by the constant pounding running that produces on bones, muscles, and joints. Below are a few of the most common injuries, their basic symptoms, and suggested treatment.

Coach's Tip: All the advice given below is very general and should be used only for educating yourself about potential running-related injuries. If you suspect that you are suffering from any injury, consult your doctor for advice on how to treat it.

Runner's Knee (Chondromalacia)

Runner's knee is caused when the kneecap begins to rub against the femur. Pain is centered in the middle of the knee, not on the side, and typically continues throughout the run and afterward. Runner's knee is mainly caused by an imbalance in the muscles that stabilize the knee, so strengthening exercises are essential to treatment. Runners who pronate (see page 16) are also susceptible to this condition, so ensuring that you are running in proper shoes is one of the first steps you should take to deal with it. Treatment also includes rest and ice, as well as the use of a brace or strap when running to help the kneecap track properly.

Achilles Tendinitis

Achilles tendinitis is the inflammation of the tendon that joins the heel and the calf. Pain is often worst first thing in the morning, dissipating throughout the course of the day. Pain may also lessen during running but returns with a vengeance after the run is over. Treatment includes rest, ice, and an anti-inflammatory medication. Stretching the tendon with heel drops (dropping the heel off the back of a step or curb) can also help, but be careful not to overstretch, which can cause further damage.

Iliotibial Band Syndrome

The iliotibial band (ITB) is a thick band of tissue that runs from the hip to the knee, along the outside of the thigh. In sufferers of ITB syndrome, the tightening of this band causes pain as it rubs at either or both of its two main connection points, the hip or the knee. Pain increases as you run, often making it impossible to continue. Rest is essential, and ice and an anti-inflammatory can help ease pain and swelling. Specific stretches to target the ITB (see page 54) can help, but avoid overstretching a sore ITB, which can cause further damage.

Plantar Fasciitis

Plantar fasciitis is the inflammation of the plantar fascia, the thick band of tissue that runs along the bottom of the foot. Pain can center around the heel or under the base of the toes. It can be most severe first thing in the morning but may lessen throughout the course of the day or during a run. A particularly stubborn injury to heal, plantar fasciitis is treated with ice, rest, and an anti-inflammatory. Prescription orthotics can also help alleviate this condition. Calf-strengthening exercises (toe rises) or picking up small objects between your toes can help stretch the fascia.

Coach's Tip: Use a frozen orange juice can to ice your plantar fasciitis. You can roll the bottom of your foot over the can, targeting the ice where the pain is worst. Also helpful is sleeping in a night splint, which you can buy at a running store or order online.

Calf Strain

Stress on the muscles of the lower legs from repetitive stress can cause pain in the calves. When a muscle is stressed beyond its ability to perform, a muscle pull results. Symptoms include pain and swelling in the affected area. Treatment involves rest to allow the muscle to repair itself and ice and an anti-inflammatory to reduce swelling. Better than treatment, however, is prevention: tight muscles are more likely to suffer from pulls. Regular stretching can help you keep them from occurring. Make sure to stretch both the calves and hamstrings, as tight hamstrings can often strain calf muscles, creating conditions for a pull. When pulls are not diagnosed and treated, they can escalate into muscle tears, a much more serious problem that requires a longer healing time.

Shin Splints

"Shin splints" is a catch-all term that can be used to refer to a number of different injuries of the lower legs. Most beginning runners suffer from some form of it, often tendinitis of the lower leg. Pain centered around the tibia (the bone running down the front of the lower leg) is the easiest symptom to recognize. Treatment includes rest, icing the affected area, and an anti-inflammatory. You can also strengthen the muscles in this area by using a towel tied around your toes to lift light weights. If the pain persists, be sure to see a doctor, as chronic shin pain can sometimes indicate a stress fracture.

TREATING INJURIES QUICKLY

The best way to handle an injury is not to ignore it. At the first twinges of pain, it is essential to recognize the symptoms of a potential injury and take steps to heal it. By quickly attending to a minor injury, you can recover with minimal lost time. Most major running injuries occur when runners ignore minor pain and continue to train through the injury. This does greater damage and usually necessitates a much longer recovery time. Use the information above to get a sense of what might be the problem, and then consult with a doctor or physical therapist to confirm a diagnosis and implement treatment.

AM I SORE OR INJURED?

One of the hardest thing for new runners to learn is the difference between being sore from training and actually being injured. The best indicator is the level of pain you are experiencing. Never ignore pain; it is the body's best gauge of the situation. If you are stiff or tender, do not hesitate to take a day off from running. If the stiffness does not go away after several days of rest or after running for a few minutes, you may have a more serious situation. If in doubt, the best thing to do is to seek appropriate medical advice.

Coach's Tip: Listen to your body. If you feel a twinge of pain that persists throughout your run, don't ignore it. Take a day or two off and let your body heal itself. But if a minor pain lessens as you run and doesn't get worse after you are finished or the next day, then you can probably continue with your scheduled training. As you become more experienced, you will learn the difference between being sore from training and being hurt.

TREATMENT OF INJURIES

Three of the main elements of treating *any* injury are rest, ice, and taking an anti-inflammatory medication. Used in combination, these methods can be effective in alleviating pain and promoting healing of common running-related injuries.

Rest

Oftentimes the best treatment of a repetitive stress injury is to remove the cause of the repetitive stress. Although many beginning runners find it difficult to break from their training schedules, it is essential to take a day or two off if you think that you may be experiencing an injury. Taking a day or two off at the first signs of injury can prevent having to take a week or two off at some point later in training.

Trying to run when injured can also cause even greater problems. When you force the body to try to run with an injury, it is forced to compensate by changing your gait or shifting weight to another part of the leg. This places stress on an area that is not used to dealing with it and can cause a second, or compensatory, injury. It is much smarter to take a few days off to allow a minor injury to heal than trying to limp through your regular runs, not only aggravating the initial injury, but also risking the possibility of causing another.

Ice

The most common treatment of minor injuries is the use of ice. Ice helps reduce swelling and inflammation by slowing the blood flow to the injured area. When the ice is removed, blood flow resumes with fresh blood, flushing the old blood, which contains lactic acid from the injury, from the area. You should ice the injured area three or four times a day, for no more than 10 to 15 minutes at a time. At the most basic, icing can be achieved by filling a watertight bag full of crushed ice cubes and applying it directly to the affected area. You can also purchase plastic gel-filled ice packs that can be refrozen for repeated use. Ice massage is most effective. Fill a small paper cup two-thirds full with water, and put it in the freezer. Once frozen, tear the paper down to expose some ice, leaving the bottom of the cup to hold. Massage the affected area with the exposed ice. Ice baths can also help. Many professional athletes have access to cold-water whirlpools in which they can soak their injured legs. You can achieve a similar benefit by filling your bathtub with cold water and adding ice. Sit in the cold water for 10 to 12 minutes, allowing the water to soak the injured area. Or, if your injury is in the lower part of your leg, you can fill a large plastic garbage can with cold water and ice and stand in it.

Coach's Tip: As much as it may sound like medieval torture, the ice bath is a wonderful way not only to treat injuries that have already occurred, but also to prevent injuries from happening in the first place. Ice baths after longer training runs (14 miles and higher) as well as one after the marathon itself can help flush lactic acid from the muscles, alleviating pain and soreness the next day.

Anti-inflammatory Medication

Since most injuries are overuse injuries, inflammation is usually involved. In such cases, the use of over-the-counter anti-inflammatory agents can help. Most anti-inflammatories belong to a family of drugs known as nonsteroidal anti-inflammatory drugs (NSAIDs). Aspirin is among the best-known anti-inflammatories and has been taken for over a century to reduce pain and swelling. Ibuprofen is another NSAID; Advil, Aleve, and Motrin are among the most common brand names. Be sure to read the label for dosage information and warnings on who should not take anti-inflammatory drugs. Overuse of NSAIDs can cause liver and stomach damage, so it is important to follow your doctor's advice if you must take an anti-inflammatory for more than a few days at a time.

Massage

Therapeutic massage can be another great way to ease the pain of an injury and, in some cases, speed its healing. Massage can help relax muscles, increase oxygenated blood flow to an injured area, and break up scar tissue that can form around an injury. Check your local yellow pages to find a certified massage therapist (CMT), preferably one who specializes in sports massage.

9

Mental Training

It has been said that the marathon is every bit as much a mental challenge as a physical one. After months of training, there is nothing you can do in the last few weeks that will significantly increase your physical preparation for the marathon. But you can begin to work on your mental preparation. Devote some serious time during the last few weeks of your training to thinking about how you will approach the race from a mental standpoint. As you ease back on the physical side of training, shift your attention to training your mind.

Positive Attitude

The most important thing that you can do to get you through 26.2 miles is to have a positive attitude. You have a choice—not just in the marathon, but in your life in general—as to how you respond to circumstances. You can choose whether you allow outside factors to control your attitude. If you are tired and running uphill into a relentless headwind, you can decide whether or not you will allow these circumstances to affect your attitude. You can choose to dwell on how tired you are or how bad you feel. But negative thoughts can draw you into a downward spiral, and soon what had been a singular frustration about the conditions can turn into an overwhelming sense of frustration and discouragement.

When you do begin to feel negative thoughts creeping in, stop yourself and consciously adjust your attitude. Push the negative thoughts out of your head and replace them with positive ones. Appreciate the beauty of the scenery or, if that's not appropriate, think about how good you will feel when you have successfully crossed the finish line. Smile at spectators along the course and thank the volunteers at the water stops. Encourage the runners around you. You will be amazed at what a difference this mental attitude adjustment can make.

For marathoners who are participating in charity running programs that have linked them with a patient, this is the best time to think about that individual and the struggles they have gone through. You have chosen to come out and do this; cancer patients or sufferers of diabetes or arthritis do not have a choice. Thinking about the pain that they suffer often puts the temporary discomfort of the marathon into perspective.

Despite these coping strategies, you may be momentarily plagued by thoughts that you can't finish. Most first-time marathoners have at least once such moment of self-doubt during the race. If and when this happens, stop and adjust your attitude. Think about all the training you have done. Have confidence in yourself that you can do this. Think about all the long miles you have put in and all the time you have devoted to preparation. You are ready for this race. Also think about all the people you've told about this challenge and how wonderful it will be to tell them that you finished.

Visualization

The mind is an incredibly powerful tool. But just as you have spent time strengthening your muscles, joints, and bones to withstand the stresses that will be put on them, you need to strengthen your mind to get you through the 4- or 5-hour-long emotional roller coaster of the marathon. One of the best ways to do this is through using mental imagery. As JoAnn Dahlkoetter, author of *Your Performing Edge*, says, "Mental training is like taking your brain to the gym."

Daydreaming is a very common form of mental imagery. Most of us spend at least a part of our day imagining ourselves doing something other than what we're doing at the moment. We reexperience events that have already happened, replaying them in our heads. We can also rehearse events that are about to occur, thinking ahead to how we might handle a particular challenge or situation. Creating this kind of mental imagery is so common for most people that they are usually not even aware that they are doing it.

When preparing for a marathon, you can take advantage of your mind's ability to imagine situations and use it to help you "train" your brain to perform during the event itself. Visualize yourself running the marathon.

A positive attitude is key to your success in a marathon.

If you have time before the event, take the marathon course map and drive the course, noting particularly challenging sections such as hills. As you are doing this, add another mental image of yourself running up over the crest of that hill, pushing forward toward the top. Also drive past where the finish line will be and visualize yourself crossing the line and look at what you see. If you are running with a particular goal time in mind, look at the clock and imagine that it reads the time you are aiming for. Add this final image to the sequence of others you have created and play them back, just like a movie, over and over again.

Mental Focus

Four or 5 hours is a long time to be doing anything, let alone something as physically and mentally demanding as running a marathon. It is sometimes easy to drift off mentally and lose concentration on the task at hand. For some first-time marathoners who choose to run races in cities away from home, the thrill of seeing new sights can also be a big distraction. Even for those running on home turf, the novelty of crowds and water stops can be enough to make even the best-known roads seem unfamiliar. Although you might welcome the chance to divert your attention from the drudgery of putting one foot in front of another, especially in the last miles, you will gain a great deal more from the marathon by focusing as intently as possible on the race itself.

Long-distance running can be an intensely spiritual experience. Part of the magic of the marathon is the heightened sense of self-awareness you gain by spending an extended period of time pushing your mind and body beyond their usual limits. Embrace the feelings—both physical and emotional—that you are experiencing, and concentrate on how they are affecting you. Triumphing over the feelings of pain or thoughts of doubt is what makes the marathon such an empowering experience. By focusing your mind, you will be able to most fully appreciate what will be one of the more incredible days of your life.

Close your eyes and actually see yourself wearing the race number and the clothes you plan to wear. Engage your other senses as well. Hear the shouts and cheers of encouragement from the crowds, feel the strength in your legs and arms and the sensation of the wind on your face. Think about emotions, too—imagine your happiness and pride as you run past the crowd and smile at them. Make as vivid a picture as you can—the more detail you add to it, the more powerful it will be.

Once you have this mental picture engraved in your head, spend a lot of time re-creating it. You can embellish it as you do so, filling in little details such as the warmth of the sun on your face or the smiles of loved ones you want to see in the crowd. Focus on this image frequently, especially right before you fall asleep at night. Also call on it whenever you start to feel anxious or nervous about the marathon. Replace any feelings of doubt or worry you might have with this familiar, well-developed mental picture of you running the race.

Coach's Tip: Wearing headphones either during the race or during training runs is a prime example of distracting focus. Although some runners—even veteran runners—swear by them, running with headphones shifts your focus away from what you should be concentrating on: your breathing, pace, and any external dangers such as traffic or other people. One of the most powerful aspects of running is the state of quiet introspection it can foster. Don't miss out on this opportunity by distracting yourself with headphones

Mental Toughness

Hand in hand with mental focus comes mental toughness. But while focus is something that you need to summon forth on the day of the event itself, mental toughness needs to be developed throughout the course of your marathon training. Remember that sweltering summer day when you just barely made it through a 16-mile run as the sun beat down mercilessly and the humidity hung in the air like a wet towel? Or

Difficult conditions can help to develop mental toughness.

that day you had to crawl out of bed at 4:30 A.M. to squeeze in a 14-miler before you flew out to a wedding that afternoon? These are the experiences that build mental toughness. You will be able to draw on these reserves during the marathon itself and benefit from the experience those miles have given you.

Mental toughness will also get you through the inevitable tough patches of the race. The marathon is filled with extremes of both joy and pain. Every marathoner experiences moments of extreme fatigue, pain, and self-doubt. In these lowest of moments, you need the mental toughness to realize the bad times will pass and that you will in fact be able to make it through to the finish. Tell yourself you are stronger than the fatigue and pain that you are feeling and that you will triumph over them. It would be easy to stop and give up without finishing, but you are tougher than that and you will endure through this bad time and make it through to the good time that you know will follow when you finish.

Dealing with Nerves

Most people experience feelings of nervousness in the days leading up to the event. This is quite normal. A lot of anticipation goes into marathon training; you have been building up for months to this one special day. When these anxious feelings begin to overwhelm you, stop and readjust your thinking. Think about how well you have trained and prepared yourself for the event. Review the number of hours and miles you have put in over the past months in preparation for it. Focus on the mental image you've created of running the marathon, and feel a sense of calm descending over you. You are ready for this, and you will do it.

Don't waste time needlessly worrying about factors that are not under your control, such as the weather. Concentrate on the factors you can control such as the pace you're going to run, your breathing, and your mental attitude. When you are able to turn your attention toward things like this that you can control, you will feel more relaxed and calm.

On the morning of the marathon, feelings of nervousness are likely to peak. These emotions usually cause physiological responses such as rapid breathing and heartbeat, "butterflies" in your stomach, or sweaty hands. You might also find that you need to use the bathroom several times before the race starts. Think of all this as nervous energy, and channel it into your running to have a better race. As JoAnn Dahlkoetter says, "You can develop the ability to feel and experience what is going on in your body and mind, and fine-tune your energy level to achieve your ideal performance state." So take a deep breath and think about focusing the nervousness toward a positive outcome. Once the marathon actually starts, most runners' nerves settle down, and they are able to concentrate on the race ahead.

Coach's Tip: A lot of times, nervousness comes from fear of the unknown. You can combat this by planning properly and giving yourself plenty of time. Make sure that you are packed and ready to leave for the race the evening before you go to bed. On race morning, get to the start far earlier than might seem necessary—this will help eliminate any nervousness about where to park, finding the toilets, and so on. By getting there before most people, you can also use the quiet time to visualize how you are going to run the race and have a successful marathon.

10

Countdown to the Marathon

The Taper

You're nearing the end of your training. You've put in the long hours and logged the hundreds of miles it takes to prepare yourself for the rigors of the marathon. The bulk of your work is done. Now you need to do something that seems almost counterintuitive: You need to rest. Studies have shown that performance is enhanced when a runner properly rests in the weeks leading up to the marathon. This period of rest and preparation is called tapering. Tapering encourages damaged muscles to heal and allows your body to store the maximum amount of glycogen in preparation for the effort it will put forth in the marathon. Follow these guidelines for tapering:

1. CUT YOUR TOTAL MILEAGE

This decrease in mileage comes primarily by shaving distance off the long runs for the week. In Higdon's schedule (see page 27), for example, after peaking with two long runs of 18 and 20 miles, you then decrease to long runs of 12 then 8 miles. The total mileage for the last 3 weeks decreases from 40 in Week 4 to 29 in Week 3, 21 in Week 2, and 9 in Week 1 (excluding the 26.2 miles of the race). Decreases such as this give your body the chance to recover from the stress it has endured as you built up your mileage in the previous weeks. But don't worry—you will not lose fitness or give up any of the gains you made during your training. You will go into the marathon rested and ready to perform your best.

2. CUT THE FREQUENCY OF YOUR ACTIVITY

You should spend less time running, for your long runs as well as shorter runs. You may also consider replacing your remaining cross-training days with rest days. You should also completely discontinue any strength training you may have been doing at this point. You need to give your body every opportunity to conserve energy and rest up for the marathon.

3. CUT YOUR TOTAL DISTANCE BUT MAINTAIN INTENSITY

Although you are reducing mileage and time spent running, don't cut back on the level at which you perform those workouts. If you normally run 9-minute miles, don't let the pace slip to $9^1/_2$-minute miles. It is the reduction of the duration of the activity that will help you prepare for the race; reducing the intensity will only hamper your race-day performance.

4. BE CAREFUL OF YOUR DIET

When you run less, you burn fewer calories. You need to carefully watch your diet to ensure the last few weeks don't result in a gain of an extra few pounds for the race. You will begin adding more carbohydrates to your diet in the week leading up to the event, but until that point, don't go overboard on the carbs. By combining tapering and carbo loading in that final week, your muscles will be able to store the maximum amount of glycogen for the race.

Coach's Tip: Be warned: This is the most dangerous period of your entire training. It will be hard for you to hold back. After months of spending hours in training, suddenly even your long runs will seem too short. You may feel somewhat let down by this. Nonetheless, you need to be well rested for the race. This is even more important if you are nursing an injury—some marathoners' best times have come when they carefully tapered due to an injury.

The tapering period is also dangerous because the stresses you have placed on your body will have weakened your immune system somewhat, and you may be more susceptible to catching a cold. Be careful when coming in contact with people who have cold-type symptoms, and wash your hands often.

The Week Before

With one week to go, continue tapering your running schedule. At this point, you need to start paying much closer attention to your intake of food and fluids as well as getting enough sleep. You also need to take care of packing and travel details related to the race itself.

HYDRATION

You don't start hydrating for the marathon on the morning of the event; you need to make sure you are properly hydrating all week long. Drink plenty of water and sport drinks throughout the week. Avoid or limit your consumption of alcohol and caffeine this week, as both of these substances act as diuretics. Carry a water bottle with you in the days leading up to the marathon. You need to be especially conscious of hydration if you fly to your event. Take a bottle of water mixed with sport drink with you on the plane, and continue to drink throughout the flight.

Drinking Too Much Water?

Recent research has revealed that drinking just water in the days leading up to the marathon and during the event itself can actually be more dangerous than dehydration. Hyponatremia is a condition in which overconsumption of water dilutes the salts and minerals in the body and may cause disorientation and, in some cases, even death. In order to prevent this condition, you can mix your water with a sports drink such as Gatorade, which contains electrolytes such as sodium and potassium. You should also use plenty of salt in your food in the two days before the race and snack on pretzels. Tomato juice also offers an excellent source of sodium. Following these simple suggestions will leave you fully hydrated and best prepared to perform to the best of your ability.

DIET

Just as you must start giving your body the fluids it needs for the event days ahead of time, you must also adjust your diet to provide it with the fuel you will need to burn during the race. This fuel comes in the form of stored carbohydrates that you should add to your diet in the week leading up to the race. You should make sure that 60 to 65 percent of the calories in your diet come from carbohydrates. Good choices include the perennial favorites, pasta and bagels, as well as whole grains, fruits, and potatoes. Snacks such as pretzels and fig bars are also good choices. But be sure not to gorge yourself; don't consume more calories than you need, rather shift the calorie sources to more carbohydrate-rich foods. If you eat too much, you will risk feeling lethargic and gaining weight.

Packing List

The following is a list of items that you should consider taking with you to the marathon. Not all items will apply to you; only pack and use clothing, equipment, or race food that you have tested in your training.

Clothing

- ❏ running shoes
- ❏ socks
- ❏ singlet or shirt
- ❏ shorts or tights
- ❏ running bra (women)
- ❏ hat or visor
- ❏ gloves
- ❏ warmup pants (bag check for postrace)
- ❏ T-shirt (bag check for postrace)
- ❏ sweatshirt or jacket (bag check for postrace)
- ❏ comfortable shoes or sandals (bag check for postrace)
- ❏ hat (bag check for postrace)
- ❏ socks (bag check for postrace)
- ❏ sweatpants (prerace disposable)
- ❏ sweatshirt (prerace disposable)

Other Items

- ❏ sunglasses
- ❏ watch
- ❏ water bottle holder and water bottle
- ❏ sunscreen
- ❏ medical tape or Nip-guards (for men)
- ❏ bug spray (if necessary)
- ❏ Runner's Lube or Vaseline
- ❏ towel (bag check for postrace)
- ❏ race confirmation (if applicable) and information
- ❏ extra safety pins
- ❏ alarm clock (don't trust the hotel's clock or wake-up call)
- ❏ adhesive bandages and antibiotic ointment (for postrace blisters)
- ❏ gels or special race food
- ❏ special race drink

REST

Getting enough rest in the days leading up to the marathon is also important. Because of nervous anticipation and an early wake-up call, you might not be able to get as restful a sleep as you might want on the night before the race. That makes getting enough sleep in the two nights prior to the eve of the marathon very important. Make a conscious effort to get to bed early enough that you can get at least 8 hours of sleep on both those nights, if possible. That way, if you can't sleep the night before the event, you'll have a bank of good sleep to draw from.

Coach's Tip: Make sure that your toenails are properly trimmed several days before the race. Don't wait until the night before, as the freshly exposed skin can be susceptible to blisters.

TRAVELING TO THE EVENT

If you will be running a marathon out of town and staying in a hotel the night before the event, it's essential to prepare everything you will need to take with you in the days leading up to your departure. If you are flying, you should pack your marathon clothes, shoes, and other race-day essentials in your carry-on luggage in case your baggage is lost or misdirected. You will also want to make sure that you have your registration confirmation, if the marathon mailed you one, and your photo ID to take with you to the packet pickup.

Make sure your race clothes are washed and ready to go well ahead of time. Do not wear anything that you have not already tested out during a training run—no new socks, hats, or sports bras, and definitely no new shoes. Check out the weather forecast for race day to help you mentally prepare for what you will be wearing. If the temperature is similar to what you've been training in, you should have no trouble, but if it is significantly hotter or colder, you may want to adjust your clothing choice. Pack several different options just to be safe. If rain is in the forecast, take rain gear only if you have used it during training. Otherwise, you will just need to accept what the day brings and make the best of it.

Prior to the race, you will likely need to walk from your hotel or car to the start of the race, and then wait around for up to an hour or longer for the race to start. If it is cool, you should take along clothing to wear over your race gear. Most races do offer an option of checking a bag of clothes that you can retrieve at the finish line, but since you'll be parting with these items prior to the race start, you should also plan to take along clothing that you can wear for the walk to the starting line. Find an old sweatshirt and pants that you are willing to part with, and just before the gun goes off, take off these clothes and drop them off along the side of the race-course. Most races have a pickup organized and donate these items to charity.

Coach's Tip: Some marathoners find that putting their names on the front of their race singlets or shirts can provide a great source of emotional support on the course. Spectators are likely to call out your name as you pass them with cries of "Way to go, Debbie!" or "You can do it, Rich!" You can use a permanent laundry marker to write directly on the fabric or, if you don't want to make it permanent, write your name on a small scrap of fabric and pin or sew it to your shirt.

The Day Before

Once you arrive at the location of the event (if you're traveling), take some time to relax and unpack. Check out the hotel and the surrounding area, but don't spend too much time on your feet. Don't forget to take your water bottle with you. If you haven't already done so, eat a wholesome, high-carbohydrate lunch. Avoid foods with too much fiber or fat content. Don't drink alcohol or caffeine during this meal.

You will also need to pick up your race packet at some point this day. Check your race information to find out where the pickup is located and how to get there. Take your confirmation and a photo ID with you. Your packet will include a bib number and, for most larger races, a plastic "Champion Chip" that you will tie to your shoe during the race to electronically record your time and pace. Race volunteers at the packet pickup will be able to give you further information about the chip and how to use it. A course map should also be included in your packet. If not, make sure to

pick one up. Most larger marathons also schedule a running expo at the location of the packet pickup, which features vendors and organizations that cater to runners. Take some time to browse the expo, but again, don't spend too much time on your feet.

Coach's Tip: No matter how tempting it may be, do not buy anything at the race expo to use in the marathon the next day. More marathon misery has been caused by runners who buy new socks or shorts at the expo, wear them the next day, and then end up with blisters or chafing during the race. The only exception to this rule would be for energy gels or sports drinks that you've already tried in training.

Once you return from the packet pickup, you may wish to go for a short run to loosen up your legs—just a very easy, 15- to 20-minute run to get the blood circulating in your legs and help ease some of your prerace nerves. You may find other marathoners in your hotel doing the same thing and have a chance to talk with them. Just don't lose track of time—20 minutes at the most at a very easy, relaxed pace. You may also want to spend some time this afternoon driving the course and familiarizing yourself with both the start and finish locations. Not only will this help ease your anxiety about the logistics of the next day, but it will also give you more details to fill in the mental picture you should be creating for your visualization routine (see page 63).

Most races also sponsor a pasta dinner the night before the marathon. This event usually features a few words by the race director and a description of the course and weather forecast. If you choose to go to this dinner, don't overload on the all-you-can-eat. Eat a sensible portion of pasta and sauce accompanied by whatever bread or vegetables are on the menu. Add a little salt to your food if it tastes like it has not been salted already. If you're eating in a restaurant or at home, choose a similar high-carbohydrate food such as rice or pasta. Again, avoid any foods that are high in fiber or fat, which can cause gastrointestinal problems on race day, and abstain from caffeine or alcohol.

After you return from the pasta dinner, relax and allow your food to digest. An hour or so before bed, you may want to have a small snack such as a cookie or muffin. Also use this time to look over race information and review your strategy for the marathon. Make sure you know how to get to the race start and the details of bag-drop. Just before you prepare to go to bed, lay out the clothes you are going to wear in the race, and pin your bib number on your shirt (fill out the emergency information on the back first). Secure your chip (if you have one) to your shoelaces according to the instructions that accompany it. Pack the bag that you plan to take to the race start with you. Once all this is accomplished, spend a few quiet moments mentally rehearsing the events of the next day, employing the visualization techniques covered in chapter 9. Breathe deeply if you feel your anxiety level starting to rise.

Once you feel calm, set your alarm clock as well a second alarm as a backup. You can also call for a wake-up call if you are staying in a hotel. You should plan to wake up at least three hours before you need to be at the race start, allowing for travel time. Don't worry if you can't get to sleep right away; just continue breathing deeply and concentrating on your visualization exercise. Lie peacefully and relax.

The Morning of the Marathon

Wake up and go through your usual morning routine. Eat the same type of breakfast you have been eating before your long runs; don't try anything new this morning. Drink a mixture of water and sport drink, and fill another bottle to take with you to the starting line. If you're not at home or haven't brought anything with you to eat, go out to get breakfast. Look out the window to check conditions, or tune in to the local radio or television weather report. Plan your day's attire accordingly.

You will also want to take care of moving your bowels before the race. Once you've eaten, drink some cold water to help encourage the process. Use the bathroom at home or in your hotel, if possible, rather than the portable toilets at the race start. Don't fret if you can't take care of this before you leave; the adrenaline you experience once you arrive at the race will likely help you take care of it soon enough. You will also need to urinate several times throughout the morning. It takes the bladder about 2 hours to clear, so drink as much as you want up to $2^1/_2$ hours before the race, then just take a small amount of water 15 minutes before the start. After all this is accomplished, take care of the last-minute details such as applying sunscreen, Body Lube, or bug spray, and get ready to go.

During the Race

Try to be at the race start at least an hour before the race is scheduled to start. This will give you ample time to drop off your bag, go to the bathroom (this alone can take up to half an hour, depending on the lines at the portable toilets), and make your way to the start. If you are running in a larger marathon, find out which corral you've been assigned to and start heading in that direction. If your race does not have assigned corrals, start back far enough in the pack that you will not be caught up in the pace of faster runners and run too fast; ask those around you for their expected finishing times and

gauge by that. If you have time, make one last-minute trip to the toilet before you enter the corral. Walk vigorously to the corral to warm up your muscles and then stretch fully once you arrive there. Bid your family and friends farewell as you prepare to start the race. Take a deep breath, remember all you've been training for, and get ready to start.

Coach's Tip: If you are running with a friend, decide before you start what your plan will be. Establish how long you plan to stay together and what you will do if one of you has to stop for the bathroom. Decide up front at which point, if any, you each will go your own way. This will avoid hard feelings and the stress of feeling that you need to either push yourself to keep up or hold yourself back to stay with your partner.

RACE STRATEGY

Once the gun goes off, start out slowly. If it's a larger marathon, you may in fact start out by walking. At the Walt Disney World and Rock 'n' Roll marathons, with nearly 20,000 participants, it can take as long as 10 minutes to even make it to the actual starting line. Don't worry—if your race is being timed by a Champion Chip, your time will not start until you cross that starting line.

Be patient in these first few miles. The adrenaline surging through your veins will make it seem as if you are running much more slowly than you are for real. It can even be a good idea to consciously try to run those first few miles a minute or so slower than you plan to run the rest of the marathon. Don't let the crowd at the start pull you out too fast, and don't try to weave in and out of people in the first half mile or so. Let the field spread out, and then settle into your pace. Be conscious of curbs and traffic cones throughout the first few miles. Run comfortably and enjoy the sheer joy of being part of a marathon.

Conserving energy is key. For the first 13 to 18 miles, the marathon should feel like a normal training run. Somewhere around Miles 16 to 18 you can start to focus on the actual racing. At this point you will still have the energy to finish strong, and may gain extra energy from passing those runners that passed you early and are now slowing down.

Pay attention to your per-mile pace times for the first few miles of the race. Most large marathons will have a clock at each mile; smaller ones sometimes have a volunteer with a stopwatch calling out times. If you are wearing your watch (and remembered to start it when you crossed the starting line), you can check your split time yourself. Be sure that you are not running too

Marathon Etiquette

Freddi Carlip, vice president of the Road Runners Club of America (RRCA), also known as "Miss Road Manners" offers an extensive list of suggestions for making race day a safe and enjoyable experience for all participants. Please read and follow these simple Rules of the Race:

At the Starting Line

1. Line up according to how fast you plan to run or walk. Slower runners and walkers should move to the back of the group.
2. Pay attention to the pre-race instructions. What you hear will not only help guide you through the course but will also keep you safe. Examples are: stay on the right side of the road, or stay inside the traffic cones, or watch the course marshals (they control traffic to make your race a safe experience) for which way to go at major intersections.
3. Pin your race number on the front of your shirt. This is where it is most visible for race officials. It will also make it easier to pull the tag off at the end of the race.
4. If you drop something just as the race starts, don't stop and pick it up—you'll endanger yourself and others. Trust that a race official will get it, or move to the side and wait until everyone has crossed the starting line and then retrieve it.

During the Race

1. Run or walk no more than two abreast. Other runners will want to get by you. If you are walking in a group, stay in the back of the pack.
2. If you are stopping at an aid station, move all the way over to the table, grab water, and move away from the table so others may get water too. If you want to stop and drink, move to the side of the road, out of the way of other runners. If there's a trash receptacle, by all means use it. If not, don't go too far with your cup. The race volunteers will be collecting the cups and will appreciate not having to go on an extended "litter patrol."
3. If you need to spit, move to the side of the road and do it there; same goes for throwing up. If nature calls, pull off the course and check for a port-a-potty or kind homeowner, or, as a last resort, a discreet clump of bushes.
4. Move to the side if someone behind you says, "Excuse me" or "Coming through." Yes, you are about to be passed and the person behind you is giving you a heads up. It's proper race etiquette to let that person through.
5. If you need to tie your shoe, or stop for any reason, please move to the side of the road. People coming up behind you are still moving and if you stop in front of them, the scene is set for a collision.
6. Feel free to shout words of encouragement to other runners. The other runners will appreciate your cheers.
7. Pay attention to what is going on around you during the race. Just as in real life, expect the unexpected. Think loose dogs, lost kids, low branches, and looming potholes.

Approaching the Finish

1. Follow the instructions of the race officials at the finish. You may be told to stay to the right or to the left.
2. Most races don't allow your nonregistered friends and relatives to run with you in a race. If a friend is running the last few miles with you, and hasn't officially entered the race, tell your friend NOT to cross the finish line. He/she should move off the race course before the finish.
3. Once you have crossed the finish line, don't stop. Keep moving to the end of the chute; stay in the exact order in which you finished. Please don't get ahead of anyone in the finish chutes. This is very important for accurate scoring.
4. Enjoy the post-race refreshments, but remember others want to enjoy the goodies too. Moderation is the key so there's food for the last people finishing the race. Don't cut in front of others. Be fair to the runners who have been patiently waiting in line.
5. Don't forget to turn in the stub on your race bib if there are random prize drawings. You've got to enter to win. Listen for the announcements.

far ahead of pace. If, for example, you run 10-minute miles during training, your split time for Mile 1 should not read 8:25. If you are running ahead of pace, consciously make an effort to slow down and get back on track. No matter how good you feel in these first few miles, if you have not trained to keep an 8:30 pace, you won't be able to pull one off on the day of the event.

Make sure to stop at fluid stations from the early stages of the race. Take a cup of water and a cup of sports drink and sip from each. Don't feel that you have to finish each cup. Toss the cups off to the side of the course if no trash barrels are provided. Volunteers will clean up the discarded cups after the race. Walk through each water station at a brisk pace. Once you take your cups of fluid, work your way back to the middle of the road so other runners can access the tables.

Try to break the rest of the marathon into parts. Each person does this differently. Some people look at it in two parts: the first 20 miles and the last 6.2. Others think of it as two halves. Some people even think of it on a mile-by-mile basis. Do whatever it takes for you to concentrate on smaller sections of the race rather than thinking of the whole thing at once. Doing this also allows you to evaluate where you are physically and mentally periodically during the race.

Eat your energy gel or the race-day food you've trained with at predetermined intervals. Most runners find that eating a gel around Mile 9 or 10 and then each 30 to 45 minutes or so after that keeps their glycogen levels topped off. Remember that you need to drink

Coach's Tip: One of the best ways to cope with the tediousness of the long miles is to create simple mental challenges, or mind games, to get you through the race. Run from telephone pole to telephone pole, focusing intently on just reaching the next one and the next, and the next, and so on. Or if you are able to carry a plastic sandwich bag with you, and your stomach can handle it, a small treat such as a Swedish Fish or Gummi Bear when you pass each mile will provide not only motivation, but also a quick sugar boost. In these ways, you can make the distance more manageable by thinking of it in very small, achievable increments rather than all 26.2 miles at once.

water with the gel, so as you see a water station coming up, open the packet and start eating the gel as you enter the water stop. That way you can also discard the gel packet along with your empty cup.

Try to keep a steady pace throughout the marathon, but don't feel bad about slowing down in the last 6 or 8 miles. Do what you need to do to get to the finish line. When you start to feel tired and discouraged, rely on the crowd to support you. Shout out to the spectators and thank the volunteers for coming out to help. If you can't muster up the energy for that, simply smile at someone. It's remarkable what a difference smiling can make. As things really begin to get tough, concentrate on the visualization techniques introduced in chapter 9. Use the power of your mind to get you through the last few miles of the race and to the finish line.

If at any point during the marathon you begin to feel dizzy, nauseated, or disoriented, stop running and seek a medical aid tent immediately. These symptoms can indicate serious problems such as dehydration or hyponatremia and should be taken very seriously. Don't let stubbornness keep you from getting the medical help you need. You can always come back and run another marathon later. If you ignore these potentially life-threatening conditions, you may not have that opportunity.

Coach's Tip: Runners are generally very friendly people. In the early and middle stages, get to know the participants who are running the same pace as you. Find out their goals, their training, and how fast they are trying to run the race. Then, when you get to that tough patch in the race that everyone seems to hit, you can help your newfound friend, or he or she may be able to help you.

The Finish Line and Afterward

Your recovery begins with your first step beyond the finish line. Keep walking after you cross the line. Volunteers will collect the stub on your bib or help you remove your chip from your shoe and give you a finisher's medal. They may also be handing out silver Mylar blankets if it's cool or cold, as well as bottles of water. Take one of each if they are available. You will have very few calories left to burn to heat your body, and you will become chilled quickly. Start drinking the water immediately. No matter how well you hydrate on the course, you will be dehydrated when you finish.

You also need to start replenishing your body. After celebrating with your friends and family for a few moments, head straight to the food area and get some orange slices, a banana, a bagel, some pretzels, or whatever they have available. Carbohydrates are most important in these first few moments after the race ends. You need to begin to replace the carbohydrates within the first hour after you finish running. Once you've taken care of these immediate concerns, if you have a minor injury such as a blister or a muscle cramp, go to the medical tent, where the personnel will see what they can do for immediate relief. If not, head to the bag pickup area to retrieve your postrace clothes and put them on. Being warm and dry will make a world of difference in how you feel.

Although your natural reaction after the marathon ends may be an overwhelming desire to sit down and rest, all the walking through the finish area to get food and gather your bag will actually help you begin your recovery. Moving will prevent your exhausted muscles from cramping up. You may also want to spend a few minutes gently stretching. Self-massage any particularly sore or tight spots such as calves or hamstrings or, better yet, sign up for a postrace massage if your marathon offers one. You can sit down at this point if you want, but don't stay seated for very long, or you may find that you can't get back up again. Once you've had a chance to celebrate with friends and cheer on any fellow marathoners, get ready to head home or back to the hotel.

Once you get back, treat any injuries or soreness that you may be experiencing with ice and anti-inflammatories. Stretch the affected area, but do it lightly and make sure you don't pull anything else. One of the very best things you can do after the marathon is to take an ice bath. This will help flush the lactic acid from your muscles and speed healing. Fill the tub up with cold water and submerge yourself up to the waist. If you can stand it, add ice to the water to further lower the temperature. Soak in the cold water for 10 minutes and then take a warm shower.

Once you are cleaned up, you may be ravenously hungry and crave "real" food, as opposed to the pasta and bagels you've been surviving on for the past few weeks. Some marathon finishers can't wait to have that juicy steak or hamburger they've been dreaming of for the last few hours of the marathon. Protein is good and will aid in muscle recovery. Some runners, however, find that they can't tolerate a large meal in the hours immediately following the race. Use your stomach as a guide and eat accordingly. Just be sure that you continue to drink plenty of fluids in the hours after the race. A good guide of hydration is the color of your urine: If it is dark yellow, you are dehydrated. Keep drinking until it is pale yellow or almost clear.

Take a nap if you wish. At the very least, you will probably want to lie down and relax for a few hours. Later in the afternoon, you will want to move again. A 15- or 20-minute walk to loosen tightening muscles is a good idea. If there is a postrace party, try to attend if you feel up to it. Not only is celebrating your achievement an important part of the experience, but the music and dancing most victory parties offer will help in your recovery. Have a great time—you've earned it!

11

After the Marathon: What Next?

Recovering from the marathon does not end in the hours following the race. In fact, your body may need up to six weeks to fully recover from the experience. What you do during these weeks will determine how quickly your body bounces back from the stresses you have placed upon it. Each person recovers at his or her own pace, and your rate of recovery from the marathon depends on a number of factors: the amount of mileage you did in your training, your age, how well you kept hydrated during the race, the weather on race day, the marathon course, and your level of fitness and flexibility.

The Week After: Rest and Recovery

The day following the marathon, you will very likely be sore. Coming down the stairs in the morning may prove to be a particular challenge. This is normal and is a natural result of the hours of pounding you put your body through during the race. Physiologically, running for such an extended time has built up a high level of lactic acid in your legs. What you need to do to start feeling better is to rid your legs of that acid. You can do so by taking a short, easy walk. Light exercise will help your body speed up the healing process. Do not run in the week following the marathon until you are sure your body is ready. In fact, it is best not to attempt any strenuous activity for three full days after the marathon. After the fourth day, if you feel up

to it, you can add cross-training activities such as swimming or cycling, but do not push too hard. Continue to use ice and take anti-inflammatories to help reduce muscle soreness and swelling.

Stretching will also help move lactic acid from the muscles. After walking for a few minutes to warm up, gently stretch the sore muscles, spending some extra time on those that are particularly tight and sore. Hot baths can also help relax tight muscles and are a good way to lead into a stretching session. A massage 24 to 48 hours after the race will also help speed recovery. Try to schedule an appointment with a certified massage therapist who has experience with sports massage, and alert him or her to the fact that you've recently completed a marathon. This will help the therapist target those areas that need the most work.

Let your body tell you what foods it needs during this period. Some people crave protein; others revert to desiring carbohydrates. You will probably be more hungry in this week than you've ever been before. Eat as a response to your hunger, and make sure your body gets what it needs. Don't forget about staying hydrated during this time, also. You may have lost up to several pounds due to fluid loss during the marathon itself. If you are properly rehydrated, your weight should return to normal within a day or so.

You also need to get plenty of sleep during this week. You may be surprised at how physically exhausted you feel. Your body is worn down and needs sleep to give it time to recover. Be aware of symptoms of colds or other illnesses that might come on during this period. This common postmarathon occurrence may be a result of your immune system being suppressed as a reaction to the stress of the marathon, or simply an inevitable result of encountering so many germs in traveling to the event or on the marathon course. Adequate sleep and a proper diet can help your immune system build itself back up.

Coach's Tip: Some marathoners have found that a good way to speed recovery after a marathon is a brisk 30- to 45-minute walk with a partner or spouse several days after the race. This not only helps to loosen the lactic acid in their legs but also gives them time to reconnect with a loved one and thank him or her for the sacrifices they made during the training period.

Getting Back to Running

Theories vary on exactly how and when you should return to regular running. Factors such as how many years you have been running and how hard you trained for the event should be taken into consideration when determining how quickly you should start running again. For first-time marathoners, the best advice is to take it easy for the first week following the marathon. Walk or do cross-training activities during those days, but do not run. After a week has passed, you should not feel more than a twinge of muscle soreness, and you will be ready to resume an easy running schedule. Start out by going for a 2- to 3-mile slow run. Gradually, over the next two to three weeks, you can build this mileage back up to a point where you are comfortable keeping it. Listen to your body, and take as many days of rest as you feel you need.

You may decide that you want to run only 15 or 20 miles per week in the months following the marathon. Many veteran runners take these months as downtime and allow their bodies to rest up for the next training season. If you've run a fall marathon, the increasingly cold weather may provide an incentive to take this well-deserved break.

Mental Recovery

Marathon recovery also has a mental component that is often overlooked. In the days and weeks that follow the marathon, you should take time to reflect on the experience and start to understand what it means to you. A large part of this process involves sharing your experience with other people. Show your finisher's medal and race photos to anyone and everyone who will look at them. Recount funny stories from the race, or recall particularly difficult moments that you were able to overcome. Sharing these experiences will help you to put them in perspective and reinforce the momentousness of your accomplishment.

But once the glow of the excitement begins to wear off, you might feel another emotion creeping in. Postevent letdown is a very common experience among marathoners, and it's perfectly normal if you begin to feel empty or even sad. You've spent the past four or more months of your life preparing for this event, and now it's over. No matter how wonderful the experience or how fulfilling it was to complete it, there is a part of us that longs for that sense of anticipation. Some people compare this to the letdown that follows a wedding or the birth of a baby. Although certainly not as severe as some cases of postpartum depression, "postmarathon blues" are very real and should be recognized and dealt with. Talk to other first-time marathon finishers about their experiences and share your feelings with them. It's more than likely that you're all feeling the same way.

Choosing Your Next Goal

Another way to help ease postevent letdown is to start thinking about how you want to move forward with your running. Do you plan to do another marathon? Or would you rather focus on a shorter-distance race? Choosing another goal—whether it is another marathon, a half-marathon, or a 5K or 10K—will help motivate you to return to running. But be realistic in your goals. A shorter race a month or two after the marathon can provide just the incentive you need to keep up with your training. For fall marathoners, Thanksgiving "Turkey Trots" are the perfect postmarathon goal races. For spring marathoners, the summer months are filled with local 5K and 10K races. Check with your local running club to find out what's coming up in your area.

The important thing is not to let the marathon be the end of your running career. It's okay if you choose never to run a marathon again, but it would be a shame if you put in all these months of training and got into such great shape and then chose not to continue running. Think of all the mental and physical benefits you've experienced in these past four or five months. Don't give them up now. Now that you've made running a regular part of your life, keep it there.

Major U.S. and International Marathons

The list below represents just a fraction of the marathons that are held every year around the world. By using the Internet you will be able to find information on these and numerous other events.

EVENTS HELD IN THE U.S.

Big Sur International Marathon: Carmel, CA; April; www.bsim.org

Boston Marathon: Boston, MA; April; www.bostonmarathon.org/BostonMarathon

California International Marathon: Sacramento, CA; December; www.runcim.org

Cincinnati Flying Pig Marathon: Cincinnati, OH; April/May; www.flyingpigmarathon.com

City of Los Angeles Marathon: Los Angeles, CA; March; www.lamarathon.com

Columbus Marathon: Columbus, OH; October; www.columbusmarathon.com

Country Music Marathon: Nashville, TN; April; www.cmmarathon.com

Dallas White Rock Marathon: Dallas, TX; December; www.whiterock-marathon.com

Detroit Free Press/Flagstar Bank Marathon: Detroit, MI; October; www.freep.com/marathon

Grandma's Marathon: Duluth, MN; June; www.grandmasmarathon.com

Harrisdirect Seattle Marathon: Seattle, WA; November/December; www.seattlemarathon.org

Honolulu Marathon: Honolulu, HI; December; www.honolulumarathon.org

HP Houston Marathon: Houston, TX; January; www.hphoustonmarathon.com

Las Vegas International Marathon: Las Vegas, NV; January/February; www.lvmarathon.com

LaSalle Bank Chicago Marathon: Chicago, IL; October; www.chicagomarathon.com

Marine Corps Marathon: Washington, DC; October; www.marinemarathon.com

Mayor's Midnight Sun Marathon: Anchorage, AK; June; www.mayorsmarathon.com

Motorola Marathon: Austin, TX; February; www.motorolamarathon.com

New York City Marathon: New York, NY; November; www.nycmarathon.org

P. F. Chang's Rock 'n' Roll Arizona Marathon: Phoenix, AZ; January; www.rnraz.com

Philadelphia Marathon: Philadelphia, PA; November; www.philadelphiamarathon.com

Portland Marathon: Portland, OR; October; www.portlandmarathon.org

San Francisco Chronicle Marathon: San Francisco, CA; July/August; www.chroniclemarathon.com

St. George Marathon: St. George, UT; October; www.stgeorgemarathon.com

SunTrust Richmond Marathon: Richmond, VA; November; www.richmondmarathon.com

Suzuki Rock 'n' Roll Marathon: San Diego, CA; June; www.rnrmarathon.com

Twin Cities Marathon: Minneapolis, MN; September/October; www.twincitiesmarathon.org

Under Armour Baltimore Marathon: Baltimore, MD; October; www.thebaltimoremarathon.com

UPMC/City of Pittsburgh Marathon: Pittsburgh, PA; May; www.upmc.edu/pghmarathon

Walt Disney World Marathon: Orlando, FL; January; dwws.disney.go.com/wideworldofsports

INTERNATIONAL EVENTS

Amsterdam Marathon: Amsterdam, Netherlands; October; www.amsterdammarathon.nl

Athens Marathon: Athens, Greece; November; www.athensmarathon.com

Berlin Marathon: Berlin, Germany; September; www.berlin-marathon.com

London Marathon: London, England; April; www.london-marathon.co.uk

Paris Marathon: Paris, France; April; www.parismarathon.com

Rome Marathon: Rome, Italy; March; www.maratonadiroma.it

Resources

BOOKS

Anderson, Bob. *Stretching*. Rev. ed. Bolinas, CA: Shelter Publications, 2003.

Applegate, Liz. *Eat Smart, Play Hard*. Emmaus, PA: Rodale Press, 2001.

Bingham, John. *The Courage to Start: A Guide to Running for Your Life*. New York: Simon & Schuster, 1999.

———. *Marathoning for Mortals*. Emmaus, PA: Rodale Press, 2003.

———. *No Need for Speed: A Beginner's Guide to the Joy of Running*. Emmaus, PA: Rodale Press, 2002.

Burfoot, Amby. *The Runner's Guide to the Meaning of Life: What 35 Years of Running Has Taught Me About Winning, Losing, Happiness, Humility, and the Human Heart*. Emmaus, PA: Rodale Press, 2000.

Dahlkoetter, JoAnn. *Your Performing Edge*. San Carlos, CA: Pulgas Ridge Press, 2001.

Daniels, Jack, PhD. *Daniels' Running Formula: Programs and Strategies: 1500 to Marathon*. Champaign, IL: Human Kinetics, 1998.

Eberle, Suzanne Girard. *Endurance Sports Nutrition*. Champaign, IL: Human Kinetics, 2000.

Ellis Joe and Joe Henderson. *Running Injury Free*. Emmaus, PA: Rodale Press, 1994.

Galloway, Jeff. *Galloway's Book on Running*. 2nd ed. Bolinas, CA: Shelter Publications, 2002.

———. *Marathon: You Can Do It*. Bolinas, CA: Shelter Publications, 2001.

Glover, Bob. *The Competitive Runners' Handbook: The Bestselling Guide to Running 5Ks through Marathons*. Rev. ed. New York: Penguin, 1999.

———. *The Runner's Handbook: A Complete Fitness Guide for Men and Women on the Run*. Reprint ed. New York: Penguin, 1996.

Henderson, Joe. *Better Runs: 25 Years' Worth of Lessons for Running Faster and Farther*. Champaign, IL: Human Kinetics, 1996.

Higdon, Hal. *How to Train: The Best Programs, Workouts, and Schedules for Runners of All Ages*. Emmaus, PA: Rodale Press, 1997.

———. *Marathon: The Ultimate Training Guide*. Emmaus, PA: Rodale Press, 1999.

———. *Smart Running: Expert Advice on Training, Motivation, Injury Prevention, Nutrition, and Good Health*. Emmaus, PA: Rodale Press, 1998.

Kowalchik, Claire. *The Complete Book of Running for Women*. New York: Pocket Books, 1999.

Noakes, Tim. *Lore of Running*. 4th ed. Champaign, IL: Human Kinetics, 2003.

Scott, Dagny. *The Runner's World Complete Book of Women's Running*. Emmaus, PA: Rodale Press, 2002.

Yessis, Michael. *Explosive Running: Using the Science of Kinesiology to Improve Your Performance*. New York: McGraw Hill, 2000.

MAGAZINES

Footnotes
(the publication of the Road Runners Club of America; available to members)
www.rrca.org

Runner's World
www.runnersworld.com

Running Times
www.runningtimes.com

WEBSITES

Active.com
www.active.com
A great resource for participants in all sports. Search for events and register online.

Cool Running
www.coolrunning.com
News and information for runners at all levels.

Dr. Pribut's Running Injury Page
www.drpribut.com/sports
Washington, D.C., podiatrist Stephen Pribut's extensive online compendium of sports injury information.

Halhigdon.com
www.halhigdon.com
Runner's World's senior writer's website with a wealth
    of valuable information for all runners.

Marathon Guide.com
www.marathonguide.com
A good resource for marathon news and information.
    Includes a full directory of U.S. marathons.

Road Runners Club of America
www.rrca.org
The national organization of road-run-
    ning clubs. Find out more about
    running clubs in your area.

Running Commentary
www.joehenderson.com
Author and columnist Joe Henderson's website with
    archives of his *Runner's World* columns and weekly
    newsletter.

USA Track & Field Road Running Information Center
www.runningusa.com
A resource for rankings, statistics, and results, as well as
    information on America's national running team.

DATE DUE

MR 2 '05			
MR 29 '05			
AP 14 '05			
AP 27 '05			
31			
16			

Demco, Inc. 38-293